LEARNING TO INVEST

LEARNING TO INVEST

A Beginner's Guide to Building Personal Wealth

by Beatson Wallace

OLD SAYBROOK, CONNECTICUT

Library of Congress Cataloging-in-Publication Data

Wallace, Beatson.
  Learning to invest: a beginner's guide to building personal wealth / by Beatson Wallace.
      p.   cm.
  Includes index.
  ISBN 1-56440-165-0
  1. Investments—United States. 2. Finance, Personal—United States. I. Title.
HG4527.W35   1993
332.6—dc20   92-33661
                                                  CIP

Manufactured in the United States of America
First Edition/First Printing

CONTENTS

Introduction, vii

CHAPTER 1 Treasury Securites, 1

CHAPTER 2 Certificates of Deposit, 9

CHAPTER 3 Money Market Funds and Accounts, 17

CHAPTER 4 Common Stocks, 25

CHAPTER 5 Reading the Common Stock Pages, 35

CHAPTER 6 Preferred Stocks, Warrants, Rights, and ADRs, 43

CHAPTER 7 The Over-the-Counter Markets, 51

CHAPTER 8 Mutual Funds, 55

CHAPTER 9 Picking Common Stocks, 67

CHAPTER 10 Bonds, 73

CHAPTER 11 Closed-end and Country Funds, 85

CHAPTER 12 Indexes, 91

CHAPTER 13 Earnings, Dividends, and Ex-Dividend, 101

CHAPTER 14 Tracking the Markets, 107

CHAPTER 15 Managing Your Investments, 115

CHAPTER 16 Keeping Records, 123

CHAPTER 17 A Widow's Dilemma, 129

CHAPTER 18 Retirement Savings, 137

CHAPTER 19 Investments to Avoid, 145

CHAPTER 20 Be Your Own Expert, 153

APPENDIX A: Federal Reserve Banks, 157

APPENDIX B: Stock Exchanges, 161

APPENDIX C: Securities Administrators, 163

APPENDIX D: National Association of Securities Dealers, 170

Index, 173

*To Judy, and any others
who want to be financially savvy*

INTRODUCTION

There is no big mystery or dark secret to the basics of investing. Anyone who is interested and capable of reading can learn the techniques simply by dissecting each potential investment step by step.

Learning to Invest has been written for the novice investor, whether an interested grade schooler, an adult, or a newly widowed grandmother. The book will dissect and explain all kinds of basic investments so that a first-timer can feel knowledgeable, comfortable, and unembarrassed.

For many years extraordinarily large sums were sitting in passbook savings accounts earning a too-modest interest simply because older depositors were afraid of the alternatives or, perhaps, still had memories of Depression stories and bank failures.

Similarly, there are younger would-be investors who neither got any financial education in school or college nor any help from parents. This intentionally nontechnical book should give investment novices of any age the confidence to start managing their own money.

How to start? The first and most important step is to decide how much risk you wish to take. This is often referred to as "the risk factor" and is summed up by the question "Are you going to lie awake nights worrying about your investment?" This is the habit of a daily trader, not a smaller-sum, first-time, longer-term investor.

If you have decided, at least initially, to take no or very low risk, there essentially are three options: U.S. Treasury securities, bank savings accounts or certificates of deposit, and money market accounts with banks, stockbrokers or mutual funds. Each of these investments will be explained in ensuing chapters.

If you have decided to assume some risk (or, perhaps, feel confident to move beyond what are termed *cash equivalent* investments of the first category), consider mutual funds that invest in common stocks of companies listed on major exchanges or trade between broker-dealers.

If income is your primary need or goal, consider the range of mutual funds investing only in preferred stocks and municipal, corporate, or U.S. government agency bonds.

After a period of mutual-fund investing during which you have become minimally familiar with financial procedures, it is time to decide whether you want to continue paying a modest annual fee to a fund manager, or whether you can handle these investments on your own.

How do you decide what stocks to select? As with mutual-fund purchases, your handpicked portfolio should be diversified and should reflect your guesses as to the chances of different companies selling more of their products or services, paying dividends, and seeing a higher price for their common stock.

First, regardless of the state of the economy, consider companies specializing in basic consumer needs, such as clothing, food, and drink; heat, light, and telephone service; and drugs and home health products. A less essential category would include all of the transportation stocks—autos, airlines, railroads, and trucking. A fast-growing industry category includes computer companies and software suppliers. The leisure industry encompasses profitable television and radio, movies, sports franchises, and sports equipment companies.

An endless combination of specific industries can be included, but the one essential is to avoid putting all your investment assets in one company, one product.

Every portfolio should have some speculative stocks, and biotechnology stocks would head that list today. Other speculative stocks would be waste management and environment control companies. Many investment advisers believe (though I don't necessarily agree) that it is essential to have about 5 to 10 percent of investable funds in precious metals.

If you are so inclined, stick to mutual funds specializing in gold or a variety of precious metals and mining company stocks. Whatever your portfolio choices, be sure to conduct personal research on the competing companies in the same industry.

If income is your major interest, consider a diversifed portfolio of utility stocks, corporate preferred stocks, bonds, or notes, and any of a large selection of so-called government-agency issues.

Utility stocks have traditionally paid dividends higher than those of most common stocks, not unusually in the 7 to 8 percent range (versus 3½ to 4 percent for established nonutility common stocks), but are less likely to yield substantial capital gains.

Corporate preferred stock and convertible and regular bonds have specific interest rates set at the time of issue so that it is possible to gear your investment for a calculated income.

U.S. government-agency issues must not be confused with U.S. Treasury securities. Too many mutual funds, intentionally or otherwise, convey the impression that their government-agency funds carry the same "full faith and credit" guarantee of principal and interest as the Treasuries. Most do not, but many investors assume they have a moral obligation to bail out these congressionally created entities if necessary. The bonds can be purchased individually or with a smaller-sum investment in a mutual fund. The better known ones are Fannie Maes (Federal National Mortgage Association), Freddie Macs (Federal Home Loan Mortgage Corporation), Ginnie Maes (Government National Mortgage Association, and Sallie Maes (Student Loan Marketing Association).

The following chapters will explain each of these investments in nontechnical language, with the hope that you will become sufficiently confident to start investing on your own without paying financial professionals to help. After all, why should they have all the fun?

1

Treasury Securities

Assuming you want to start with supersafe investments, the best are U.S. Treasury securities. Initial investments in Treasuries *(T-Bills)* are available for a range of sums and maturity dates.

Three-month (sometimes referred to as thirteen-week) T-Bills and six-month (twenty-six-week) T-Bills are normally auctioned every Monday, except when a federal holiday falls on a Monday, in which case the offering normally takes place on a Tuesday. One-year (fifty-two-week) T-Bills are normally auctioned on the fourth Thursday of the month. These all require an initial investment of $10,000, with additional increments of no less than $5000 each permitted.

Treasuries with longer maturities are called *Notes* and *Bonds.* The T-Notes have maturities of two to ten years. The two- through six-year T-Notes require an initial investment of $5000, while the seven- through ten-year Notes can be obtained for $1000 each. The T-Bonds are all issued in $1000 increments and have maturities ranging from eleven to thirty years. The thirty-year T-Bonds are most often referred to as *bellwether* Treasury rates in newspaper and broadcast reports, which simply means that they are the long-range yardstick from which all lower interest rates are estimated.

Any of these Treasuries can be purchased through a brokerage house or a bank, currently for a fee of about $50, or directly, without cost, through one of the nation's twelve Federal Reserve Banks. (See Appendix A for the address and telephone number of the Federal Reserve Bank serving your area.)

The Federal Reserve System handles the security auctions for the U.S. Treasury Department. Whenever the government needs more money for budget bills or has to pay off maturing securities issued earlier, the Fed schedules new auctions. The Monday and Thursday auctions are routine and regular; dates for the others are announced in advance once a quarter by the Treasury.

Most of these billion-dollar Treasury issues are bought by what are called *institutional investors*—brokers, mutual funds, insurance companies, banks, etc.—which submit competitive bids of no less than $500,000. Their bids include a high and low range of specific interest rates. When all of the winning bids are tabulated and accepted by the New York Federal Reserve Bank, an average rate is set and announced in late afternoon of the auction day.

This is the interest rate to be paid to all noncompetitive investors—those who submit bids for no less than the minimum initial sums. There are no winners and losers in the noncompetitive category, which normally comprises no more than 10 percent of the total issue—all are accepted. When the noncompetitive interest rate is published in the next day's newspapers, two rates are usually quoted. The first is the actual interest to be paid on the T-Bill, and the second is the higher annualized rate, which represents the earnings that would accrue if the same principal were invested for a full year. This simply helps the investor compare the T-Bill earnings with comparable investments for which an annual percentage rate is always quoted.

Paper certificates of ownership were once issued and mailed within days of the auction to all investors. If invested through a broker or bank, the company would have one certificate for its total winning bid, and its bookkeeping department would assign a specific dollar amount to each client's account. The remainder would be held in the firm's account for trading until final maturity in what is called the *secondary market*. Every day billions of dollars of Treasury securities actively trade between institutional investors. The long columns of figures published daily in *The Wall Street Journal* under the heading *U.S. Treasury Bonds, Notes, and Bills* are the going rates for trading in this secondary market.

Now ownership of all Treasury securities is recorded only in *book entry* form. This simply means the Treasury (or a stockbroker or a mutual fund) has an entry on its books showing that you own a certain dollar amount of securities (or bonds), and a statement of this ownership is sent to you periodically. While the new system is more complicated initially, it is certainly much safer than mailing out certificates, which could be stolen or lost. And at maturity time, the certificates no longer have to be mailed back to the disbursing Fed bank and a negotiable check issued and mailed. The Fed also claims that this new Treasury *Direct* system is more efficient and saves the government millions of dollars.

How does Treasury *Direct* work? For those buying Treasuries through a broker or a bank, there is essentially no change. But an individual investor must first open a Treasury *Direct* account and have a permanent account number assigned. This application can be requested by telephoning or visiting the nearest Fed (see Appendix A). The uncomplicated, single-page form asks three types of questions: name, address, and Social Security number; the name and the Federal Reserve district account number of your commercial bank (the numbers at the top right corner of your checks); and your bank's routing transit number, which is assigned by the American Banking Association (the numbers at the bottom left of the checks). If you use a savings bank, it will provide the appropriate numbers.

Once the Fed assigns you an account number, usually within a week or ten days for the round-trip mailings, subsequent transactions are handled instantly by computer transfer, and records of your transactions are kept by the Treasury's Bureau of Public Debt. Once this has been done, you are ready to make your first Treasury security investment.

Each issue has its own color-coded application form. You can get these by phoning or writing to the local Fed, and overnight mailing is promised. Each filing of a noncompetitive bid must be received by noon of the auction day, or if sent by mail, must be postmarked by midnight of the previous day and include a certified check for $10,000, $5000, or multiples of $1000, depending on the issue ordered. If a bid is not received by the deadline, the application will be held over until the next auction of a similar issue; if none is scheduled, the application and check will be returned.

The T-Bills are sold at a discount from the par, or the face maturity value. For instance, if the noncompetitive rate is set at 6 percent, the $10,000 investment will actually cost only $9,400, and on the third day after the auction, $600 (the difference between the $10,000 you paid up front and the discount price) will be credited to your account at the bank you

Q Is it possible to purchase zero-coupon bonds directly from the Federal Reserve?

A No. The U.S. Treasury occasionally designates some securities as "strippable," meaning that the individual brokerage houses or mutual funds sell the zero-coupon certificates and the interest coupons separately. *The Wall Street Journal* publishes a daily list of the trading prices in the secondary market of these Treasury Note and Bond Strips. The list designates the trading price for these separate issues by *np* for the note principal; by *bp* for the bond principal; and by *ci* for the stripped coupon interest. Each entry includes the month and year of maturity, the buy and sell prices, and yield based on those prices.

designated when you applied for the Treasury *Direct* number. In effect you are receiving your interest payment in advance, and on the maturity date your account will be credited with the full $10,000 originally invested.

With an original T-Bill application, you may elect to have the $10,000 rolled over into another issue of the same maturity period for a maximum of up to two years. For example, thirteen-week bills can be rolled over eight times; twenty-six-week bills four times; and fifty-two-week bills twice. If you have not designated reinvestment, the Treasury will send a notice of the pending maturity forty-five days in advance, with instructions for reinvesting. If you don't respond, the $10,000 will automatically be paid out, and you will have to submit another noncompetitive bid.

Similarly, separate bid forms are required for investments in T-Notes and Bonds. These, though, are sold at either discount or premium to par (the face maturity value), depending on the average of the noncompetitive bids. Since the interest-payment checks are credited to your account every six

CHART 1

Securities

This chart for the regular Monday auction of $10,000 Treasury bills appears in many Tuesday newspapers. The only key figures for the investor are 1) the average price (what the noncompetitive bidder pays) and 2) the coupon equivalent rate.

In this example, the investor pays $9,909.30 and earns 3.59 percent for a thirteen-week bill, and pays $9,815 and earns 3.66 percent for a twenty-six-week bill. The coupon equivalent figures show what the same sums would earn if reinvested at those rates for a full 365-day year, simply to compare with the current annual bond rates.

Similar charts for Treasury notes and bonds are published whenever those auctions occur.

	13-Week	26-Week
Applications	$45,291,530,000	$38,636,805,000
Accepted bids.................	$11,738,830,000	$11,726,235,000
Accepted at low price	10%	28%
Accepted noncompet'ly ...	$1,384,100,000	$1,003,785,000
❶ Average price (Rate)	99.093 (3.59%)	98.150 (3.66%)
High price (Rate)	99.095 (3.58%)	98.160 (3.64%)
Low price (Rate)	99.090 (3.60%)	98.150 (3.66%)
❷ Coupon equivalent........	3.67%	3.78%
CUSTP number..............	912794ZM9	912794ZX5

Both issues are dated July 2. The 13-week bills mature Oct. 1, 1992, and the 26-week bills mature Dec. 31, 1992.

Treasury notes and bonds trade after the original auction date in what is called the secondary market. These trades are in large-sum lots between investment bankers, mutual fund managers, and brokers. Brokers, in turn, will sell these Treasuries in smaller-sum lots to individual investors at prices reasonably close to these quoted figures. Here's what the columns of figures mean:

1—The annual interest rate on the face value of the security.
2—The month and the year the security matures. When two years appear, this indicates an alternate refinancing date.
3—The "Bid" and "Asked" figures are the approximate highest and lowest prices offered between buyer and seller.
4—The "Bid Change" is the difference between yesterday's and the previous day's mid-afternoon prices. The prices are quoted in hundreds with the decimals representing thirty-seconds.
5—The "Ask Yield" figure is what you will earn if the security is held to maturity based on the asking price, not the par value.

❶	❷	❸		❹	❺
	Maturity				Ask
Rate	Mo/Yr	Bid	Asked	Chg.	Yld.
8⅞	Nov. 97n	111:01	111:03	+ 6	6.40
7⅞	Jan 98n	106:15	106:17	+ 8	6.45
8⅛	Feb 98n	107:18	107:20	+ 6	6.49
7⅞	Apr 98n	106:12	106:14	+ 7	6.52
7	May 93–98	101:01	101:09	− 2	5.48
9	May 98n	111:22	111:24	+ 5	6.56
8¼	Jul 98n	108:04	108:06	+ 6	6.58
9¼	Aug 98n	113:01	113:03	+ 6	6.62
7⅛	Oct 98n	102:20	102:22	+ 8	6.60
3½	Nov 98	96:16	97:16	+75	3.95
8⅞	Nov 98n	111:07	111:09	+ 6	6.67
6⅜	Jan 99n	98:12	98:14	+ 7	6.67
8⅞	Feb 99n	111:08	111:10	+ 7	6.73
7	Apr 99n	101:18	101:20	+ 6	6.70
8½	May 94–99	106:00	106:08	+13	4.97
9⅛	May 99n	112:19	112:21	+ 5	6.79
8	Aug 99n	106:18	106:20	+ 7	6.81
7⅞	Nov 99n	105:24	105:26	+ 5	6.86
7⅞	Feb 95–00	104:11	104:15	+13	6.01
8½	Feb 00n	109:06	109:08	+ 5	6.92
8⅞	May 00n	111:13	111:15	+ 5	6.96
8⅜	Aug 95–00	106:16	106:20	+11	6.02

Chart reproduced by permission from the Associated Press.

months, your first interest payment will be corrected to include either fractionally more or less than the stated semiannual coupon rate. All subsequent payments on January 1 and July 1 will be half of the annual rate.

Interest on all Treasury securities is fully taxable by the federal government but tax-exempt by the states. T-Bill investments made during the last quarter won't be taxable income until the following year, when the full $10,000 is paid.

For a comprehensive but nontechnical explanation of Treasury *Direct* and Treasury Bills, Notes, and Bonds, send $4.50 to the Federal Reserve Bank of Richmond, P.O. Box 27471, Richmond, VA 23261 for a copy of James F. Tucker's "Buying Treasury Securities at Federal Reserve Banks." If you are interested in the mathematics of Treasury security interest rates, write to the Public Information Department, Federal Reserve Bank of New York, New York, NY 10045 and ask for free copies of "fedpoints 7" (*Understanding U.S. Government Securities Quotes*) and "fedpoints 28" (*How to Compute Returns on Treasury Issues*).

2

Certificates of Deposit

Uncle Sam's safety net extends to most Certificates of Deposit, more familiarly known as CDs. A CD is simply a loan to a financial institution for an agreed period of time at a guaranteed interest rate.

The majority of the popular investment CDs are issued by banks, others by credit unions and brokerage houses. CDs are insured if they are issued by banking institutions that are dues-paying members of the Federal Deposit Insurance Corporation (FDIC) or the National Credit Union Association (NCUA). Both are independent, federally created entities with deposit guarantees increasingly assumed by Congress and recent executive administrations as government obligations—up to certain limits.

Those limits were once $100,000 per single account, with slight variations for separate joint and trust accounts. Since the onset of savings and commercial bank failures in the late 1980s and excessive taxpayer–financed federal bailouts that have continued into the 1990s, there has been much discussion and numerous legislative proposals to establish new limits. Those favoring CD investments should stick to the $100,000 standard maximum guarantee and be alert to any changes in the regulations.

The interest rates paid on CDs can vary from one bank to another in the same city, or from one region of the country to another. At one time Texas banks were struggling to stay afloat and were offering the highest rates in the country to attract deposits. Similar efforts to lure deposits have since been noticeable in other sections of the country. Basically the rates are negotiable, depending on the size of the deposit and/or the length of time the invested sum will be left on deposit.

Most banks have a set menu of CD offerings, starting with weekly, quarterly, semiannual, and so on, through whatever number of years a depositor wishes to gamble on a fixed interest rate. If you think interest rates will fall, lock up a CD at today's rates; if you think rates will rise, stay short term so you can reinvest without paying a penalty. The decision is a guess, even for the experts.

Typically, the weekly rate would be a fraction of 1 percent higher than the current *federal funds rate* (the rate banks pay one another for overnight borrowings to balance their books) or the current *discount rate* (what banks pay to borrow from the Federal Reserve System). The quarterly, semiannual, or annual interest rates are all adjusted regularly and routinely fluctuate up or down with the Treasury security auction rates, plus or minus whatever difference the bank can pay out and still be competitive with neighborhood banks or more distant banks soliciting CD deposits through extensive national advertising to promote their rates and arrange transfers.

There are significant characteristics of CDs that need to be understood. The interest income is normally not paid

Q Why does the "prime" have such importance when determining what other interest rates, such as those on certificates of deposit, will be?

A The prime rate is said to be the lowest rate commercial banks offer to their most creditworthy customers. In reality, it is just a handy benchmark for other interest rates banks pay and charge.

There are three interest rates that are interrelated: First, the *discount rate*, or what the Federal Reserve Bank charges on loans to member banks. These loans are made at an interest cost of about half of the current prime rate, but there are limits on the amount and for the time period that these borrowings can be outstanding.

Second, when banks cannot borrow more of these lower-cost funds from the Fed, they must borrow from other banks (with surplus funds) to balance the books under regulatory requirements at the end of each day. These loans are for a few *basis points* (one hundred basis points equal 1 percent) higher than the first-mentioned discount rate and are called the *federal funds rate*.

Third, if a bank has to borrow from the Fed or other banks with surplus cash and pay certain interest rates on deposits to stay competitive, this is, in effect, its *wholesale cost of money*. Its retail price is the current prime rate, the benchmark from which all other consumer/client loans are set.

Q Is there a publication that compares prevailing interest rates for certificates of deposit?

A The one most widely published in the financial press is called "100 Highest Yields" and is issued weekly by Bank Rate Monitor (P.O. Box 088888, North Palm Beach, FL 33408). The interest rates are tabulated only for federally insured certificates of deposit issued by both commercial and savings banks. For a modest charge anyone can subscribe to this publication.

until maturity; hence, a set interest is quoted, with a higher annual percentage rate representing the compounding of accumulating interest. If you specify in advance that you want these payments on a more frequent schedule, such as monthly or quarterly, the total annual earnings will be proportionally less than if the earnings on the invested sum were left to maturity. In other words, if you select an alternate payment option, the interest earnings will be lower.

Interest earnings are taxed by the federal government and your state of residence. Some states exempt CD earnings from taxation if the issuing bank is incorporated in that state but fully tax earnings from out-of-state banks. Other states, including Massachusetts, tax bank interest earnings at a lower rate than the usual corporate dividend and interest rate. In some locales, such as New York City and Philadelphia, the city, in addition to the state, taxes these earnings.

Earlier it was mentioned that investments in insured bank CDs could be handled through a broker. What actually happens is that the broker deposits a large sum in specific banks paying a better-than-average interest rate and then parcels it out to clients in lots of less than $100,000 so that each account gets under the FDIC guarantee umbrella. (Suggestions have been made to disallow these so-called brokered accounts, but to date they still are legal.)

It is inevitable that the guarantee regulations will change. In the meantime keep your account totals and any CD investment—principal plus expected interest earnings—under $100,000. For example, if you expect to earn 8 percent on a CD through to maturity, invest no more than $92,000 in that particular bank. If you have more to invest, choose another bank.

Under present FDIC procedures, if a bank is taken over, either it will be liquidated or its assets will be turned over to a stronger bank. If it is liquidated, insured deposits will be paid in full, often as speedily as within three days. Similarly, any sums invested in CDs will be paid back promptly, but interest accumulation will cease as of the liquidation date. If the troubled bank is taken over, checking or savings account balances will automatically be transferred, and the client will have the option of staying with the successor bank or transferring the funds to another bank. CDs will also be transferred to the successor bank, but the old interest accrual rate will be subject to negotiations: If the old rate was excessively high by current market rates, expect to be offered a lower rate to maturity or the chance to withdraw the funds entirely without penalty.

If the total of all accounts exceeds the maximum FDIC or NCUA coverage, the excess balance will probably be tied up for many months while the insuring agencies and/or the successor banks pay off creditors. Even then there is no guarantee that anything will be paid on excess deposits.

Some states, though, have legislatively created state guarantee funds. These privately operated corporations assess member dues to build payoff assets. In the event of a bank or credit union failure, the federal insurance covers the first $100,000 and any excess deposit is covered by the state insurance fund. Such funds sound airtight and are so advertised. In practice, as many bank depositors in Ohio and Maryland found out this past decade, there is never enough money in the guarantee coffers to cover all such deposits. A sensible policy is to avoid having any deposits in excess of federal insurance guarantees in any one bank or credit union.

CHART 2

Certificates of Deposit

Every Wednesday the Bank Rate Monitor, a financial services and research company in North Palm Beach, Florida, compiles a list of bank interest rates coast-to-coast. Local newspapers have this list tailored to their own circulation area and publish this list on Thursdays, the same day that the *IBC/Donoghue's Money Fund Report* (see chapter 3) is printed. The accompanying chart gives the figures for several accounts in the Greater Boston area in mid-August 1992.

The first two columns of figures show interest rates on sundry savings and checking accounts.

The third, fourth, and fifth columns show the slightly higher rates paid if the deposits were committed to a longer term (6-month, 1-year, and 2½ year) to maturity. Individual banks will tailor CDs of any amount and duration a depositor wants. In each case, different banks would assess varying penalties if the CDs were not left on deposit to the specified maturities.

The second to last line, labeled "Boston average," permits the reader to compare the ten listed banks' rates with their own or other banks in the area.

Similarly, the last line permits a comparison with similar bank interest rates elsewhere in the country. The Bank Rate Monitor compiles these figures by surveying the one hundred largest banks in the ten largest markets.

Bank money market accounts

Here are annual effective yields on money market accounts and certificates of deposit offered by some Boston-area banks and thrifts on Wednesday. Yields are based on the method of compounding and the rate state yesterday for the lowest minimum deposit required to open an account. Minimums may vary from bank to bank. Higher yields may be offered for larger deposits. CD rates are for fixed rates only. All figures are percents.

	Money market accounts	Super NOWs	6-month CD	1-yr CD	2½-yr CD
Bank of Boston	2.94	2.02	3.25	3.44	3.96
Bay Bank	3.04	2.02	3.10	3.45	4.07
Fleet Bank of Mass.	2.84	2.02	3.20	3.46	4.08
Shawmut Bank of Boston	2.79	2.02	3.15	3.51	4.24
State Street B&T	2.53	1.92	3.25	3.75	4.50
Boston 5 Cents Savings	3.04	2.27	3.30	3.66	4.44
Eastern Bank	3.04	2.78	3.56	3.82	4.59
Neworld Bank	2.94	N.A.	3.25	3.55	4.07
Provident Institute for Savings	2.89	2.02	3.15	3.56	4.13
South Boston Savings Bank	3.35	3.35	3.60	4.18	4.86
Boston average	2.94	2.30	3.28	3.64	4.29
Bank Rate Monitor Index*	3.03	2.32	3.28	3.56	4.33

SOURCE: Bank Rate Monitor, N. Palm Beach, Fla. 33408

Chart reproduced with permission from
Bank Rate Monitor, North Palm Beach, FL 33408

3

Money Market
Funds and Accounts

M oney market mutual funds and accounts are available in many varieties. Banks call them *money market accounts*; brokers say *money market sweep accounts*; and most investment companies managing a family of mutual funds offer *money market funds*.

Credit the mutual fund industry for creating these ingenious investments back in the early 1970s. In twenty short years total assets under management have increased steadily to more than $580 billion, according to the Investment Company Institute, the Washington-based mutual fund industry's lobbying group. And whenever the stock market is in turmoil, the total sum invested in money market funds and accounts either skyrockets or plummets. In effect investors are liquidating stock portfolios and "parking" the sums for another day when the money will go back into stocks and bonds.

Back in the days when interest rates on bank savings deposits were restricted by federal regulations, mutual fund managers saw the billions of dollars of savings deposits earning low and fixed interest as an irresistible pool. They designed an investment package with very little or no minimum, a modest administrative charge, and free check-writing privileges that permitted the investor to withdraw as little or as much as desired instantly. Later, more imaginative features were added, such as automatic payment of a client's monthly mortgage, utility bills, etc., from the money-fund balance.

These mutual fund investments are spread over a variety of different issues, such as corporate short-term notes. By tradition, and now by Securities and Exchange Commission (SEC) fiat, the portfolios have no more than 5 percent of any one issue, except for those invested 100 percent in U.S. Treasury securities. More recent money funds have been tailored with portfolios of single state or national tax-exempt bonds. Each portfolio has a specific number of days to maturity, normally averaging in the mid-fifties with a maximum of ninety days.

The short maturity of these fund portfolios has been the secret of their safety, even though only the bank funds are covered by federal insurance. To date no mutual fund or brokerage money market client has lost money. In the few cases of money-fund default or liquidation, management (or an acquiring management) has made up the losses, sometimes with the help of the Securities Investor Protection Corporation. (The SIPC is a federally created but privately operated organization—sort of the FDIC of the brokerage and mutual fund industry—that insures all fund and brokerage accounts up to $500,000.)

Regardless of who the sponsor is, shares in a money market mutual fund or a bank money market account are each worth $1.00, and the accumulating interest changes daily for the mutual fund accounts, or periodically, say once a week, for bank and brokerage accounts. The interest on the mutual

Q My $82,000 nest egg is invested in bank savings accounts. I plan to use this to purchase a home. Unfortunately, the interest earned results in some hefty taxes. What other interim investment could I consider that would protect the principal, be immediately available, and be tax-free?

A One good alternative would be a tax-free, same-state money market fund. By same-state I mean issued by a municipal entity of the state in which you pay income tax. Many brokerage houses and mutual-fund sponsors offer these investments. It is even possible during an era of low bank account and CD interest rates that your total tax-exempt return would be significantly higher than taxable interest. The principal amount invested may vary, depending on the value of the underlying short-term municipal issues, but not enough to cause concern. Most of these portfolios mature in less than sixty days, too short a time for any precipitous changes in interest rates.

fund accounts is calculated when the various markets close in mid-afternoon and the underlying portfolio is valued.

From the outset the mutual fund money market interest rates have been tabulated by *Donoghue's Money Fund Report* and are now published weekly by the successor British parent company, *IBC/Donoghue's Money Fund Report* of Ashland, Massachusetts. The weekly *Donoghue's Report* is compiled late Wednesday and published in many major newspapers on Thursday or the following Sunday. The basic report figures published by the newspapers are total dollar value of assets under management, the average maturity of the portfolio in days, the seven-day average yield, and the seven-day compounded yield for projecting an annual percentage rate, or comparative coupon yield.

The weekly subscription copy ($595 annually) includes the more important specific information on the percentages of each issue in the fund. Since June 1991, reflecting the SEC change of rules, the taxable-fund-portfolio breakdown has included two rating tiers. The first tier designates holdings rated A-1 plus or A-1, and the second tier holdings require a rating of A-2 or its equivalent by any of the five "Nationally Recognized Statistical Rating Organizations." These include Standard & Poor's, Moody's, Fitch, Duff & Phelps, and the International Bank Credit Analysis (IBCA). In cases where a fund has not paid for a rating by one of these agencies, its board of directors must certify that the issue has an equivalent standing.

Here are the definitions for percentage breakdowns of taxable funds listed in the *IBC/Donoghue's Money Fund Report:*

- U.S. Treasury bills and notes guaranteed by the full faith and credit of the U.S. government;

- U.S. (other) government-agency obligations backed by the moral obligation of the U.S. government;

- Repurchase agreements collateralized by U.S. securities or prime instruments and held by the fund until repaid. (A repurchase agreement is a short-term contract under which the seller of a security agrees to buy it back at a fixed price while the buyer holds the Treasury security as collateral.);

- Time deposits that are nonnegotiable and are maintained in a domestic or foreign bank with any second-tier holdings identified;

- Domestic bank obligations: negotiable certificates of deposit and banker's acceptances (loans made to cover products shipped but not yet paid for) that are first-tier or second-tier securities as defined by the SEC;

- Foreign bank obligations: Eurodollar certificates of deposit, Yankeedollar certificates of deposit, or banker's acceptances that are first tier or second tier (*Eurodollars* are deposits held by overseas branches of U.S. banks; *Yankeedollars* are deposits held by U.S. branches of foreign banks.);

- Commercial Paper (borrowings by corporations and banks) with separate listings for first-tier and second-tier holdings of short- and/or medium-term corporate notes;
- FRNs: Floating Rate and Variable Rate notes (usually tied to a specific Treasury issue) that are first-tier or second-tier securities;
- Total second-tier holdings refers to the percentage in all previous eight categories of investments with this rating.

As you can see, these specifics give a complete picture of the risk a money market mutual fund takes with its (and your) investments.

The IBC/Donoghue's Report also lists portfolio statistics for tax-free funds but gives little detail beyond identifying the percentage of "rated" and "unrated" municipal short-term issues in each fund. The SEC has said it is reviewing this category with an eye to requiring a similar first- and second-tier rating system.

Brokerage houses holding clients' stocks or bonds in *street name* (meaning the broker has title to the certificates and allots ownership of a certain number of shares to each client's account) now maintain money market fund *sweep accounts* for cash credited from the sale of stocks and bonds and being held for later reinvestment, and same-day crediting of interest and dividends received from corporate payers. Previously these sums were either mailed to the client or held as idle cash until requests for new investment purchases were received. Now these sums earn money market interest from the moment they are credited. The same money market funds are

CHART 3

Money Market Funds

There are three distinct types of money market funds. The first has a mixed portfolio of corporate short-term money issues with the interest income subject to federal and state tax. The tax-free funds of municipal issues come in two categories: ones with interest exempt from federal tax but taxed by the states; and ones exempt from both federal and state tax if the portfolios contain only single-state issues and are sold to residents of that state.

1—The fund name, often incorporating part of the managing company name.
2—The total dollar amount of the fund's assets.
3—The average number of days to maturity of all issues in the portfolio.
4—The average yield of the portfolio for the past seven days.
5—The compounded yield for the past seven days, often indicating some issues matured and were replaced with ones earning higher or lower interest.

All three of the funds in bold face are managed by Merrill, Lynch Inc., the investment house with the largest amount of money fund investments. Its Cash Management Account (CMA) Money Fund at this date had $27.8 billion in the fund, more than half invested in corporate commerical paper. This income is federal and state taxable. Income from the CMA Tax-Exempt Money Fund ($7.5 billion in assets) is exempt from federal tax. The CMA PA (for Pennsylvania) Municipal Money Fund is doubly tax-exempt for residents of that state.

Taxable

❶ Fund	❷ Assets ($ million)	❸ Average maturity (days)	❹ 7-day average yield (%)	❺ 7-day compound yield (%)
Mass Cash Mngmnt Trust	456.4	62	3.0	3.1
McDonald Money Market Fund	280.8	89	3.2	3.2
McDonald US Government MMF	150.4	78	3.5	3.6
Merrill Lynch CBA Money Fund	1,268.2	80	4.0	4.1
Merrill Lynch CMA Government	4,244.1	77	3.6	3.7
Merrill Lynch CMA Money Fund	**27,627.9**	**87**	**3.7**	**3.7**
Merrill Lynch Government	1,372.6	57	3.6	3.6
Merrill Lynch Institutional	2,008.1	60	3.7	3.8
Merrill Lynch Ready Assets	8,171.2	86	3.6	3.6
Merrill Lynch Ret Res MF(r)	6,551.4	85	3.5	3.6
Merrill Lynch Treasury Fund	293.6	53	3.4	3.4
Merrill Lynch USA Govt Res	581.0	79	3.2	3.3
Metlife - State Street MMF	174.2	46	3.3	3.3

Tax-Free

Fund	Assets ($ million)	Average maturity (days)	7-day average yield (%)	7-day compound yield (%)
CMA NC Municipal MF	210.1	72	2.1	2.2
CMA NJ Municipal MF	336.9	72	2.4	2.5
CMA NY Municipal MF	584.6	84	2.3	2.4
CMA OH Muncipal MF	190.8	67	2.4	2.5
CMA PA Municipal MF	**246.9**	**40**	**2.4**	**2.4**
CMA Tax-Exempt MF	**7,559.1**	**81**	**2.5**	**2.5**
CT Daily Tax Free MMF Income Fund	168.9	42	2.1	2.2
California Tax-Free MMF	109.4	33	2.3	2.4
Calvert Tax Free Reserve CA Port	313.3	14	3.0	3.1
Calvert Tax Free Reserves MM	1,670.7	14	3.1	3.1

Chart reproduced with permission from IBC/Donoghue's
Money Fund Report of Ashland, MA 01721.

available to any nonbrokerage client. In fact, Merrill Lynch for some time has topped the money-fund list for the largest sum—currently some $55 billion—under its several money-fund managers.

When bankers belatedly realized that their traditional low-interest savings depositors were withdrawing money and investing in mutual fund and brokerage accounts paying appreciably higher interest rates, they, too, began offering accounts paying the higher money market rates. A bank money market account is a similar but different animal. It does carry FDIC protection, which mutual funds do not, of $100,000 total for all accounts in that bank. The money is generally used for the standard banking business of consumer, mortgage, or real estate development loans, and the interest earned is arbitrarily pegged to some changing benchmark interest rate, such as the weekly Treasury Bills, or whatever rate other local and regional banks are paying.

Interest earnings from all three varieties of money market accounts are taxed by the federal government, states, and some localities. Among the tax-free funds, single state funds (with portfolios issued by entities in your state of domicile) are not taxed at all. Tax-exempt funds with a mixed portfolio of several state issues are federally exempt, but the portion of earnings from out-of-state issuers is taxable by your own state. The exception is a portfolio with issues from Puerto Rico and Guam or other such U.S. territories; these are also fully exempt.

This ends our discussion of *cash equivalent investments*, so-called because in most circumstances they can be readily cashed in. We will now discuss the more complicated common stocks.

4

Common Stocks

C ommon stocks are the heart of corporate finance and an investor's dreams of fortune. They are risky, but not even small fortunes can be accumulated without some risk, and the risks can be minimized. More importantly, stock investments are the best way to keep pace with inflation.

In a technical sense a common stock represents a proportional piece of the ownership of a company. In a practical sense it is only a chance to share in any dividends declared or profit from any capital gain if the shares are sold. In reality only those owning or controlling 51 percent or more of the outstanding shares can say they have a voice in a company's operations and destiny. Sometimes that majority needs proxy voting help to hold on; more often management does as it pleases.

At the birth of a company, management does and should have full say. Invariably "management" includes the inventors, the engineers, or the businessmen who saw a chance to offer a better, cheaper product or service. These company visionaries provided the startup money and sweat, or persuaded family, friends, bankers, and venture capitalists to contribute. At this stage each participant usually gains control of a certain percentage of the enterprise and its capital shares.

Once a company is established and success seems possible, there is always a need for more operating, marketing, or research funds. To raise these funds management offers shares to the public. When the company was organized its articles of incorporation authorized the issuance of a certain number of shares. More than a majority are usually allotted to the principals, and the remaining number are held by the company treasurer as *authorized but unissued shares.*

These are the first shares to be registered with the Securities and Exchange Commission (SEC), the federal investment regulator, and the National Association of Securities Dealers (NASD), the industry group that has jurisdiction over stock brokers and tracks certain markets. Then all or part of a stock issue is offered for sale to the public.

By this action a company and the investment bankers handling the initial public offering (IPO) establish what they think the dollar value of the stock should be. Once the IPO is completely sold and market trading begins, the public buyers control the stock price. The issuing company benefits only from the sale of the first public offering or any subsequent stock issues.

Few new stock issues are listed and start trading on an exchange. Many are never listed, simply because they fail to meet listing requirements or are so infrequently traded that listing is a useless and unnecessary expense. The New York Stock Exchange (NYSE), which celebrated its 200th birthday in 1992, has the strictest listing requirements and highest

Q What does *par value* mean in reference to stock certificates?

A In the case of common stocks, according to the New York Stock Exchange rules, par value has little relationship to the market value of stock. It is merely a dollar amount assigned to issued shares by the company's charter for balance-sheet accounting. In the case of preferred stock, it signifies the dollar value on which dividends are figured.

Q What are the advantages for a stockholder when the company declares a split? The stock value remains the same; only the number of shares increases.

A Initially the split shares do trade for the same total price as the original presplit share, but management hopes that the new lower share price will make its stock accessible to more investors and create more daily trading volume. Invariably, in time, the stock price does increase, and an investor can sell the split shares for a capital gain and still hold the original investment. Some companies routinely declare share splits in lieu of dividends on the theory that retained earnings are better used for product and plant than distributed to shareholders.

entry fees. Hence, the companies with stock trading there are considered the most financially stable. These companies when first listed must have:

- 1.1 million common shares publicly held (excluding management-owned shares), with a market value of $18 million;
- net tangible assets (property, manufacturing equipment, inventory, etc.) of between $9 million and $18 million, with $18 million the current norm; and
- pretax earnings of $2.5 million for the most recent year and

$2 million pretax for each of the two preceding years, or an aggregate for the last three fiscal years of $6.5 million, with a minimum in the most recent fiscal year of $4.5 million. All three years must be profitable.

The entry fee for a company's initial NYSE listing is $36,800. Then there is a separate assessment for each million shares: for the first 1 and 2 million shares, $14,750 per million; 3 and 4 million, $7,400 per million; 5 to 300 million, $3,500 per million; and 300 or more million, $1,900 per million. In addition there is an annual minimum fee of $14,630 per million based on the first and second million, and $750 for each additional million.

Recently the NYSE had 2,077 companies qualified for listing of 2,007 common shares, 573 preferred, and 16 warrants and 4 rights, with a total market value of $3.8 trillion.

The American Stock Exchange, once known as Curb Market Traders because the brokers traded year-round outside on Wall Street sidewalks, was officially organized in 1953. Then and now the AMEX, as it is routinely called, has been considered the midsized growth-company marketplace. Its basic stock listing requirements are:

- 500,000 shares with a minimum of 800 public shareholders. Prior to listing the shares must have a minimum trading price of $3.00 each with a market value of $3 million;
- net tangible assets of at least $4 million; and
- pretax earning of at least $750,000 in the last fiscal year, or in two of the last three fiscal years.

The AMEX also has alternate minimum listing requirements for newer companies with extraordinarily high expenses for research and development.

Recently the AMEX included listings for 843 companies

with 971 shares of common, preferred, and warrants, with a market value of $103.3 billion.

The intial entry fee for AMEX companies is $5,000, plus a schedule of fees similar to that of the NYSE, based on per-million shares listed. This starts at $5,000 for 1 million or less; $10,000 for 1 to 2 million; on up to $122,500 for 75 to 100 million. The annual exchange fees are also based on total shares, starting at a minimum of $4,500 for 1 million or fewer, and rising per million to a maximum of $12,500 for any number in excess of 16 million.

The third and fastest-growing marketplace for trading company stocks is the NASDAQ National Market System (NMS), organized in 1982 and supervised by the National Association of Securities Dealers (NASD with the initials AQ—for Automated Quotations—tagged on). This trading is done entirely on a broker-to-broker basis by electronic computer network and telephone. (Chapter 7 will discuss other NASDAQ securities not included in the National Market System.)

The listing requirements for the NASDAQ National Market System stocks are:

• At least 500,000 shares held by no fewer than 800 public shareholders, with a market value of $3 million and trading for no less than $5.00;
• net tangible assets of $4 million;
• pretax income (in last fiscal year or two of last three fiscal years) of $750,000 and net income for the same periods of $400,000; and
• at least two market makers (brokerage houses that maintain continuous bid-and-ask trading in the stock).

The initial listing fee for NMS stock companies is $5,000, plus $25,000 for 1 to 5 million shares; $37,500 for 5 million to 15 million; and a maximum of $50,000 (including the original $5,000) for any number of shares in excess of 15 million. The NMS annual participation fees start at $2,000, plus the per-share increment, rising to a maximum of $8,000.

Recently the NASDAQ National Market System included 2,679 domestic common stocks, 67 foreign securities, and 35 preferred, with a market value of $507.7 billion.

As you can see by comparing the diffferent listing requirements, entry fees, and annual fees, it is easier and cheaper for a company to have its stock trade on the NASDAQ, but that isn't the only reason for its growing popularity. Any number of well-financed companies with stocks trading actively could qualify for either of the other stock exchanges but prefer the NASDAQ market. The managements of two such companies, Apple Computer and MCI Communications, have said they prefer to have a market maker in every brokerage office coast-to-coast, rather than relying solely on a specialist on a stock exchange floor.

In the near future, when global stock trading is the norm rather than the exception, there is little doubt that a NASDAQ sytem will be the more popular prototype.

In the meantime, on any given day, the NYSE processes the largest volume of all U.S. stock trades, but these do not all occur on the exchange floor in New York City. Company stocks qualified for listing on the so-called Big Board also trade regularly on five regional stock exchanges (Midwest in Chicago; Pacific, with trading floors in Los Angeles and San Francisco; Boston; Philadelphia; and Cincinnati) and through electronic networks operated by NASD for direct broker-to-broker trades, and Instinet, for certain block trades between institutional investors, such as investment bankers and insurance companies.

In addition to being convenient local conduits for trading stocks listed on the New York and AMEX exchanges and the NASDAQ systems, the regional exchanges play a significant role in helping smaller startup companies.

None of these companies could qualify for listing on any major exchange, but selling their first public stock in their own backyards to knowledgeable neighbors and investors often leads to ultimate success.

The five major regional exchanges all have trading floors similar to the NYSE and AMEX, with the same flurry of shouted orders and paper-littered floors circled by the electronic trading screens, with their continuous streams of changing stock-price quotes.

Selected local brokers route orders for Big Board and AMEX stocks by direct-line phone and computer terminals to their brokerage representatives on the exchange floors in New York City. They are simultaneously taking orders by electronic networks for any local companies allowed to list with only minimal requirements.

The total number of all swaps in ownership of NYSE-listed stocks is reported as the *composite* trading volume, or more usually given in a chart labeled *Trading in NYSE Stocks* or *Volume by Exchanges*.

This is not the figure flashed on your television screen or included in stock market story headlines. Those inaccurate, but routinely used, figures represent only trading at the NYSE on Wall Street. Similarly, the traditional Dow Jones up or down figures quoted are unrepresentative of the day's stock market action. They represent trading only in thirty well-known company stocks listed on the NYSE and omit the day's action in 2,254 other NYSE issues as well as fifty percent more of trades in stocks listed on the American Stock

Exchange, the NASDAQ system, and nowadays even the same stocks trading on other exchanges around the world where, not invariably, the prices will differ.

For instance, on April 17, 1991 the Dow Jones Industrial Average (DJIA) closed for the first time in its history above 3,000 (actually at 3004.46), and all the media reports heralded this heavy trading day. The thirty DJIA stocks with total trading volume of 32.7 million shares got all the headlines, but actually all NYSE-listed stocks accounted for the heavy volume. The real day's trading figures for all exchanges were:

Boston—5.0 million;
Cincinnati—2.1 million;
Instinet—198,500
Midwest (in Chicago)—13.7 million;
NASD—17.7 million;
NYSE—246.9 million;
Pacific (in Los Angeles and San Francisco)—10.6 million; and
Philadelphia—3.9 million

All told some 300.4 million shares of NYSE-listed stocks traded, but only the 246.9 million traded on the Big Board were acknowledged. Similarly, if you were reading or hearing about the Big Bang stock market day, little or no mention was made of the 267.5 million other shares trading on the same day on the NASDAQ National Market System, or the 16.5 million shares traded on AMEX.

Paradoxically, the NYSE price-trading charts provided by the financial wire services and printed in your daily newspaper use volume figures—high, low, and last prices—reflecting trading on all U.S. exchanges, not just those occurring in New York. Hence, these charts are labeled *Composite Transactions*, meaning nationwide trading.

Equally meaningless are the daily quotations in the financial press, on the radio, and on television to the effect that the "average stock" gained (or lost) X cents. Sometime, as an experiment, total the daily figures for your own stocks and see how they compare with the average gains or losses. The difference will surprise you.

Any novice intent on becoming a serious investor needs to understand and be able to interpret the many market charts presented on the daily financial pages. That's the subject of our next chapter.

Note: All listing, market value, and annual fee figures were provided by information persons at the New York Stock Exchange, the American Stock Exchange, and the National Association of Securities Dealers and reflect third-quarter 1992 information.

5

Reading the
Common Stock Pages

Knowing how to read the stock quotation pages is the essential starting point for any novice investor. Once understood, these pages of stock names and numbers unlock many mysteries.

Unfortunately, few metropolitan newspapers can afford or have a readership sufficiently interested to devote more than the minimal space and limited figures to these daily reports. The one exception is *The Wall Street Journal*, which professionals consider the bible of the daily financial press and which necessarily offers the most complete tables in a print size more easily read than those in other papers. Hence, the following explanations are based on chart samples from the *Journal*.

First, though, you need to know which exchange table to check for a company you are interested in. The best and easiest source is the Standard & Poor's *Stock Guide*, published and updated monthly. Alongside each company name is the trading (or ticker) symbol and market as well as a full range of financial data.

Traditionally, all stock-price figures are quoted in dollars and eighths of a dollar (12½ cents) or multiples of those figures. Here's how to get through the stock-page maze.

The first two columns of figures are labeled *52 Weeks, Hi Lo* and the numbers represent the highest and lowest prices paid for the stock during the previous fifty-two weeks, plus whatever number of trading days there have been in the current week.

The next two columns name the stock and give its ticker symbol. (If you see the initials *vj* in front of the name, this indicates that the company is in bankruptcy or is being reorganized.) Some of these wire-service abbreviations (usually necessary so that as many letters as possible fit in the column width) are nearly incomprehensible, while others are relatively transparent. For instance, *AmHomePdts* means American Home Products with a simpler ticker symbol of *AHP*, while an *AmT&T* listing for American Telephone & Telegraph with a ticker symbol of *T* can readily be recognized by almost anyone. After a while you'll become familiar with these financial hieroglyphics. The trading symbol for the company is the correct and efficient way to identify a stock on a broker's order slip (or if the broker is ordering a trade via a computer or telephone).

The next heading, *Div*, gives the cash dividends in dollars and cents paid in the past calendar or fiscal year for each share. If you divide this sum by four, you should get the correct figure for the usual quarterly payment. If there has been an increase (or decrease) in any one quarter, this will not be an equally divisible sum. If there is a blank here, it means no dividend has been paid.

The *Yld* % column tells you what the income from the stock is worth at today's trading price. For example, if the

Q Why are stock-market fractional price quotations always given in eighths?

A A learned Boston Latin–Harvard College associate has suggested that this fraction represents the "pieces of eight" that equaled one of the old Spanish dollars. A spokesman for the New York Stock Exchange said they were unable to nail the origin precisely, but their amateur historians agreed that early American stock trading, long before exchange days, was carried on in Spanish dollars; hence the fractions were in eighths, or today's 12½ cents.

stock's trading price closed that day at $25.00 and it pays a $1.00 annual dividend, the yield would be 4 percent.

The *PE* number is an abbreviation for *price/earnings ratio* and is computed by dividing the day's trading price by whatever earnings-per-share figure the company reported for the past twelve months. These numbers are considered by some market technicians as irrefutable evidence of a stock's value. A too-high figure (some say above twenty) means it's time to sell (or, at least, not to buy), and a low figure (some say below ten) is supposed to be the magical signal to buy. The trouble is, this number is based on past earnings and does not necessarily give any hint of present and future earnings.

Next we get to the heart of yesterday's trading. The first column is labeled *Vol 100s* and the numbers tell you the total shares traded. To sandwich long numbers in the limited space, sales figures are quoted in hundreds, so you must add two zeros to the number printed. This figure represents all the trades of one hundred shares (a round lot) or more. The exact total would include any odd-lot trades, those representing less than one hundred shares, but these never get counted except as total odd-lot trades reported separately.

Sometimes a *z* appears in front of the sales figure. This means the figure printed represents total sales, not the usual hundreds.

Sometimes an *x* appears in front of the sales figure, meaning that a stock is *ex-dividend*, or that the date has passed for the buyer to receive the most recently declared dividend. (For a detailed explanation, see chapter 13.)

The next three columns, headed *Hi*, *Lo*, and *Close*, give the price range for the day's trades. These numbers don't necessarily mean what you should have gotten if you sold stock or what you paid if you bought, but your price would have to fall within these high and low figures.

Sometimes a letter is printed alongside the closing price. This means that the final closing price represented a trade occurring on an exchange other than the New York Stock Exchange, by brokers who are not members of the NYSE. These letters and the trading places are:

a—American Stock Exchange (the AMEX) in New York City.

b—Boston Stock Exchange.

c—Cincinnati Stock Exchange.

g—NASD, the National Association of Securities Dealers, who conduct Over-the-Counter trading in NYSE-listed stocks.

k—Instinet, a direct computer trading network used by institutions, such as investment bankers, insurance companies, and mutual funds, for buying large blocks of shares without routing the orders through an exchange-floor specialist.

p—Pacific Coast Exchange, which maintains trading floors in

Los Angeles and San Francisco and regularly trades for thirty minutes after the 4:00 P.M. closing time in New York.

u—Midwest Stock Exchange in Chicago.

x—Philadelphia Stock Exchange.

The Wall Street Journal recently added some convenient symbols to the left of its stock charts that provide helpful signals for the investor. Chief among these are arrowhead symbols, pointing up for a new high in the stock price, down for a new low; an *n*, meaning that the "hi" and "lo" figures are for the period since a new issue was listed (not the normal fifty-two-week spread); an *s* for stocks recently split or a stock dividend declared; and an *x* for a stock trading that day ex-dividend. (When a stock is split by the company, each holder receives more shares without any immediate increase in value. The theory is that the lower per-share price will attract more investors and, ultimately, if a stock selling for $100.00 per share is split 4 for 1, the new per-share trading price will be $25.00. It is more likely that an individual investor could buy a one-hundred-share lot for $2,500 rather than the much higher $10,000 cost of the old pre-split shares.)

These explanations have covered only the common stocks. There are other categories of stocks included in these tables for the NYSE, the AMEX, and the NASDAQ National Market System. They are trading quotations for preferred stocks, warrants, and rights listed below the common-stock prices of the issuing company, and American Depositary Receipts (ADRs) for shares of foreign companies, all discussed in the next chapter. In addition, you will find quotes for closed-end mutual funds explained in chapter 11.

CHART 5

Reading the Common Stock Pages

The Wall Street Journal uses an identical format for reporting daily trading in common stocks listed on the New York Stock Exchange, the NASDAQ National Market System, and the American Stock Exchange. Here's the formula:

1—Fifty-two weeks high and low trading price range, including the most recent market day.

2—The stock issuer, e.g., ARCO Chemical Co., mostly owned by Atlantic Richfield Co. Other stock listings are name abbreviations.

3—The trading symbol, RCM.

4—The annual dividend ($2.50) based on the last four quarterly cash payments.

5—The percentage yield (5.4 percent) based on the day's share price divided by the dividend.

6—The price-to-earnings ratio is the stock price divided by earnings per share for the last twelve months.

7—Day's trading volume in hundreds; add two zeroes to 185 for total of 18,500 shares.

8—The day's high, low, and closing per-share trading prices.

9—The net change in price from previous market day close.

	❶		❷	❸	❹	❺	❻	❼		❽		❾
	52 Weeks					Yld		Vol				Net
	Hi	Lo	Stock	Sym	Div	%	PE	100s	Hi	Lo	Close	Chg
					-A-A-A-							
	16⅞	10⅝	AAR	AIR	.48	3.7	16	106	13	12⅞	12⅞	– ⅛
	11⅝	10⅛	ACM Gvt Fc	ACG	.96	8.6	...	815	11⅛	11	11⅛	...
	10⅜	8⅞	ACM OppFd	AOF	.80	8.3	...	187	9⅝	9½	9⅝	...
	11¼	9⅜	ACM SecFd	GSF	.96	8.7	...	2928	11	10¾	11	+ ⅛
	9½	8⅜	ACM SpctmFd	SI	.79	8.7	...	526	9⅛	8⅞	9⅛	+ ⅛
	9⅝	8	ACM MgdIncFd	AMF	.95	10.0	...	897	9⅝	9⅜	9½	...
	12⅞	10⅝	ACM MgdMultFd	MMF	1.08	9.4	...	79	11¾	11½	11½	– ⅛
	2½	1⅜	ADT wt			...	...	1175	2	1¾	1⅞	+ ⅛
n	9½	5	ADT	ADT		...	...	9315	8¾	8⅜	8¾	+ ⅜
	32⅞	20¼	AFLAC	AFL	.44	1.5	16	746	30⅜	29¾	30⅛	+ ⅜
	26	15	AL LabsA	BMD	.18	.8	93	101	23⅛	23	23⅛	– ⅛
	2⅛	¾	AM Int	AM		...	...	134	1	15/16	15/16	– 1/16
	12	3⅜	AM Int pf			...	...	264	3¾	3⅝	3¾	...
	11¾	10⅜	AMEV Sec	AMV	1.05	9.3	...	65	11⅜	11¼	11¼	...
	80¼	54½	AMR	AMR		...	...	4313	65	64⅛	64½	– ⅛
	47	**34½**	**ARCO Chm**	**RCM**	**2.50**	**5.4**	**23**	**185**	**46⅞**	**46⅛**	**46⅜**	**– ⅜**
	2⅜	1	ARX	ARX		...	...	10	1¾	1¾	1¾	...
	56	40¾	ASA	ASA	2.00	4.6	...	684	44⅞	43¾	43⅞	– ¾
s	34¾	24⅜	AbbotLab	ABT		...	24	19755	33	31¼	31½	– 1¼
	14⅝	12	Abitibi g	ABY	.50	...	...	20	13½	13½	13½	+ ⅛
	6¼	3⅜	AcmeElec	ACE		...	13	52	4⅞	4⅝	4⅝	– ⅜
	11¾	5½	AcmeCleve	AMT	.40	5.6	...	182	7¼	7⅛	7⅛	+ ⅛
	37⅜	18⅞	Acuson	ACN		...	14	415	22¼	21⅞	22¼	+ ¼
	20¼	17⅜	AdamsExp	ADX	1.63e	8.6	...	169	18⅞	18¾	18⅞	...
	21½	8⅜	AdvMicro	AMD		...	6	4620	15½	15⅛	15¼	– ⅛
	49⅛	31¼	AdvMicro pf		3.00	7.5	...	88	40	40	40	+ 1

Chart reproduced with permission from the Associated Press.

6

Preferred Stocks, Warrants, Rights, and ADRs

More than 90 percent of the daily stock charts represent trades of common stocks. The other 10 percent or less are trades in preferred shares, warrants, and rights, all issued by companies with common stocks trading, closed-end mutual funds (see chapter 11), and what are called ADRs, American depositary receipts for ownership of shares in foreign companies whose common stocks trade on exchanges in the parent countries.

Unlike common stock, on which a dividend may or may not be paid, a preferred stock is issued with a guaranteed annual dividend (hence the name *preferred*). If the issuing company omits a common-stock dividend, the preferred-stock dividend must be paid or accumulate to be paid later before any common dividends will be paid again.

Similarly, if a company is reorganized or goes out of business, the preferred stockholders are first in line with other creditors, while the common-stock shareholders get very little, or even nothing.

The individual preferred issues, usually issued at different times as the company needs money, are identified either by initials (e.g., *pfA*, *pfB*, *pfC*,) or simply by *pf* followed by the dollar-and-cents amount of the fixed dividend.

Most preferreds continue trading without any specified redemption dates. Some preferreds have a specific call (or redemption) date; others require the company to set aside a fixed dollar amount annually in a sinking fund (funds held separately from other company assets) to redeem all of the issue at once or a portion of the total each year. Still others can be converted into common shares at a fixed price and/or by a certain date.

The preferred with a convertible feature can be issued and traded publicly, with daily prices reported in the regular stock lists, or privately, with no trading or regular reporting of value, except by estimating the conversion ratio into common stock and the exercise or effective date. In recent years the preferreds not publicly traded were obtained by large-sum private investors or investment bankers who helped the company beef up the balance sheet, ward off unwelcome takeover attempts, or, in the case of banks, to meet capital requirements.

One important reason companies issue preferred stock is that the fixed dividends are considered to be a cost of doing business and therefore are a deductible pretax item, while common-stock dividends are paid out of the post-tax net earnings.

Warrants are very similar to convertible preferreds. They are issued with a specific time span during which an investor can buy shares of common stock at a certain price. Depending on the current stock price and the exercise date and ratio, warrants usually trade for a fraction of the current market value of the common stock.

Q What is the difference between preferred and common stocks?

A The dividend on a preferred stock is established when issued, is guaranteed, and must be paid before any dividend is declared for the common stock. More importantly, under present tax law, preferred dividends are considered a deductible cost of doing business and, in this respect, are similar to debt and can be deducted from earnings before any profits are distributed to common shareholders. Consequently, should the company ever be declared bankrupt, preferred shareholders have a legal claim on any remaining assets, while common stockholders get nothing.

Q Do the warrants issued to me when British Petroleum Co. PLC bought the Standard Oil Co. stock it did not already own have any value?

A British Petroleum shares are listed and trade on the London Stock Exchange. Each of the company's ADRs (American depositary receipts), listed and trading on the New York Stock Exchange, represents twelve of the ordinary shares trading in Europe. When BP bought out Standard Oil, it paid the U.S. stockholders $71.50 per share in cash and gave them one warrant for each share tendered to buy BP ADRs at $80.00 a share until December 31, 1992. At the time of the takeover, BP ADRs were trading at around $70.00 each, and it seemed a good bet that the shares would be trading for more than the $80.00 offer so that warrant holders could buy more shares at a bargain price. Consequently, the warrants were trading for as high as $8.00 each. In subsequent months BP stock fell to the mid-$40s and the warrants to less than $1.00 The warrants trade daily and are listed with the common stock as BritPetrol wt. If the stock has not recovered to more than the $80.00 exercise price by the deadline, no one will want to buy more shares and the warrants will expire useless. It is also possible that BP could set a new expiration deadline.

A startup company issuing its initial public offering (IPO) will often offer a certain number of warrants per common share as an inducement to buy the stock.

Rights serve much the same purpose. Since warrants or rights permit a stockholder to buy more common stock at below-market prices, they have a market value of their own and actively trade. These trades are included in the regular stock charts. Warrants and rights can readily be identified in the charts by the initials *wt* or *rt* immediately after the company name. Since most have an expiration date, an investor otherwise not interested in acquiring more shares should sell the warrants or rights for the trading price, which usually becomes higher as the expiration date nears.

A newer version of rights cropped up in the late 1970s and continued through the 1980s. These could be called "defensive" rights and are neither issued nor traded. They merely exist as authorized but unissued shares legally a part of each share of common stock as a defense against a takeover opposed by management and directors. In effect, these rights authorize a common stockholder to buy more common stock at a much lower price than the current market price. It is reasoned by management that the sudden purchase of many shares would discourage any hostile takeover by making it more expensive, and perhaps impossible, to gain majority control.

A brokerage statement that includes common stock with these defensive warrants will show a notation as follows: *w/rts to pur c/stk under certain circumstances*, meaning "with rights to purchase common stock under certain circumstances"—such as a takeover attempt.

Trading quotations for American Depositary Receipts (ADRs) are sprinkled alphabetically through the stock charts.

These entitle the investor to ownership of a certain number of shares in a company normally trading, say, in London in pence or Tokyo in yen. For example, British Petroleum Company, one of the world's leading oil producers, has its ADRs trading on the NYSE, and each ADR represents twelve shares of the common stock trading in London. Similarly, ADRs for Sony Corporation, the electronics and entertainment giant, also trade on the NYSE, but these are equal to one common share listed on the Tokyo Exchange.

No stock certificates are issued to ADR investors. They are held by a trustee bank, either in the parent country or in New York City, which maintains street-entry statements of ADR ownership, much the same as a brokerage account. Dividends, often paid semiannually by foreign companies, are paid in U.S. currency and are subject to normal federal and state taxes. If the parent country of the ADR has a mandatory tax on dividend income, credit for any withheld sum can offset normal U.S. tax liability.

Recently there were ninety-seven common and preferred stock ADRs trading on the NYSE, forty on NASDAQ's National Market System, and eight on AMEX.

CHART 6

ADRs, Preferred and Warrants

This is the same chart displayed in chapter 5 to explain common stock listings. Now we'll pinpoint other names sprinkled through these listings, which represent different investment issues.

1—ADT is the name of ADT Ltd., a British company that provides security alarm systems and conducts auctions of used cars. This listing is for the company's American depositary rights. Since this was a new listing on the NYSE, there were no reportable figures for the dividend, percentage yield, and PE columns.

Immediately above ADT, you see a line labeled "ADT wt" ("wt" stands for warrant). On April 23, 1992 these warrants were issued to then shareholders (one warrant for each six commonly owned). The warrants entitle the holders to buy one ADT common share for $10.00 beginning July 1 through to June 30, 1994. In the meantime, the warrants actively trade.

2—H.F. Ahmanson is considered the nation's largest holding company for savings banks and mortgage lending companies. The second listing here is for its preferred shares (designated by the "pf"), which pay a fixed dividend of $2.40, representing a yield of 9.1 percent at this day's closing price of $26.50.

Chart reproduced with permission from the Associated Press.

-A-A-A-

	52 Weeks Hi	Lo	Stock	Sym	Div	Yld %	PE	Vol 100s	Hi	Lo	Close	Net Chg
	16⅞	10⅝	AAR	AIR	.48	3.7	16	106	13	12⅞	12⅞	− ⅛
	11	10⅛	ACM Gvt Fc	ACG	.96	8.6	...	815	11⅛	11	11⅛	...
	10	8⅞	ACM OppFd	AOF	.80	8.3	...	187	9	9½	9⅝	...
	11¼	9	ACM SecFd	GSF	.96	8.7	...	2928	11	10¾	11	+ ⅛
	9½	8	ACM SpctmFd	SI	.79	8.7	...	526	9⅛	8⅞	9⅛	+1⅛
	9⅝	8	ACM MgdIncFd	AMF	.95	10.0	...	897	9⅝	9	9½	...
	12⅞	10⅝	ACM MgdMultFd	MMF	1.08	9.4	...	79	11¾	11½	11½	− ⅛
❶ n	2½	1	**ADT wt**			...	...	1175	2	1¾	1⅞	+ ⅛
	9½	5	**ADT**	**ADT**		...	...	9315	8¾	8	8¾	+
	32⅞	20¼	AFLAC	AFL	.44	1.5	16	746	30	29¾	30⅛	+
	26	15	AL LabsA	BMD	.18	.8	93	101	23⅛	23	23⅛	− ⅛
	2⅛	¾	AM Int	AM		...	...	134	1	15⁄16	15⁄16	− 1⁄16
	12	3	AM Int pf			...	...	264	3¾	3	3¾	...
	11¾	10	AMEV Sec	AMV	1.05	9.3	...	65	11	11¼	11¼	...
	80¼	54½	AMR	AMR		...	...	4313	65	64⅛	64½	− ⅛
	47	34½	ARCO Chm	RCM	2.50	5.4	23	185	46⅞	46⅛	46	−
	2	1	ARX	ARX		...	...	10	1¾	1¾	1¾	...
	56	40¾	ASA	ASA	2.00	4.6	...	684	44⅞	43¾	43⅞	− ¾
s	34¾	24	AbbotLab	ABT		...	24	19755	33	31¼	31½	−1¼
	14	12	Abitibi g	ABY	.50	...	...	20	13½	13½	13½	+ ⅛
	6¼	3	AcmeElec	ACE		...	13	52	4⅞	4⅝	4⅝	−
	11¾	5½	AcmeCleve	AMT	.40	5.6	...	182	7¼	7⅛	7⅛	+ ⅛
	37	18⅞	Acuson	ACN		...	14	415	22¼	21⅞	22¼	+ ¼
	20¼	17	AdamsExp	ADX	1.63e	8.6	...	169	18⅞	18¾	18⅞	...
	21½	8	AdvMicro	AMD		...	6	4620	15½	15⅛	15¼	− ⅛
	49⅛	31¼	AdvMicro pf		3.00	7.5	...	88	40	40	40	+ ¼
	9⅛	2⅞	Advest	ADV		...	...	10	6	6½	6½	...
	71¾	54¾	Aegon	AEG	3.88e	5.7	6	3	68¼	68¼	68¼	...
	47	31⅞	AetnaLife	AET	2.76	6.8	8	1781	41⅛	40½	40⅞	+ ¼
	12⅛	7½	AffilPub	AFP	.24	2.2	20	1588	107⅛	10½	10¾	+ ¼
n	25¾	21½	AgriMinl	AMC	2.42	10.8	...	219	23⅛	22½	22½	−
❷	20⅞	12	**Ahmanson**	**AHM**	**.88**	**4.8**	**10**	**5440**	**18¼**	**17¾**	**18¼**	**+ ¾**
	26⅝	24	**Ahmanson pf**		**2.40**	**9.1**	**...**	**140**	**26½**	**26**	**26½**	**+ ⅛**
	22½	7	Aileen	AEE		...	7	116	7	7⅛	7¼	...
s	49½	30½	AirProduct	APD	.80	1.7	20	983	46¼	45½	46⅛	+ ⅛
	30	14	AirbornFrght	ABF	.30	1.8	14	899	16⅝	16¼	16⅝	+ ⅛
	32½	14	Airgas	ARG		...	29	537	31⅞	31	21¾	+
	13¾	8⅛	Airlease	FLY	1.68	15.8	8	146	10⅝	10¼	10⅝	− ⅛
	25	23⅝	AlaPwr pfA		1.90	7.9	...	41	24	23⅞	24	...
	11	9¾	AlaPwr pf		.87	8.2	...	16	10¾	10⅝	10⅝	...

7

The Over-the-Counter Markets

While most stock news centers on the trading of shares through the New York and American Stock Exchanges and the NASDAQ National Market System, the largest and fastest-growing markets are what are traditionally called Over-the-Counter (OTC) Markets. There are literally thousands of such stocks outstanding; no one knows precisely how many are available or trade this way.

The companies may be very small, with a limited number of shares outstanding. Some may be privately held or have a very small number of shares held by the public. Others may be companies once dead, now active.

More often, transactions in these stocks are direct sales between brokers who negotiate *bid* and *ask* prices.

Not too many years ago such transactions were all handled in person or by telephone; nowadays they are handled by electronic computer networks. An interested buyer flashes a *bid* price, and a seller responds with an *ask* price. The high and low range of the two prices is called the *spread*. The negotiated trading price will be generally somewhere between the two.

Most of these trades are tabulated by the National Quotations Bureau, and the prices are delivered every business day to subscribing brokers on what are called the *pink sheets*. (Similar data are available on *yellow sheets* for corporate bond transactions.)

Once this was the only way to get price quotes on infrequently traded stocks. Today pink sheets are more of a reference guide for OTC brokers to locate a market maker for the stock of a certain company and get a ballpark idea of any recent stock-trading ranges. To get a more up-to-date price, the broker will phone the market maker or signal the firm by computer network.

The major OTC computer network is operated by the NASD and covers two different stock issues: those not yet qualified for the NASDAQ National Market System (about 2,100 stocks) and commonly reported as NASDAQ Small Cap (for capitalization) market stocks; and about 4,000 pink-sheet stocks whose market makers voluntarily report daily to NASD's OTC Bulletin Board either actual transaction prices or the current bid and ask figures. (The OTC Bulletin Board is a computer-screen service allowing member firms to enter, update, and/or view quotation information on OTC securities that are not eligibile for listing on NASDAQ—or may have been deleted—or pink-sheet securities voluntarily supplying stock data.)

Those on the NASDAQ Bid and Ask stock table must have:
common-stock issue publicly held of 100,000 shares;
total assets of $4 million;

Q How does one find the addresses of companies with stocks trading on the Over-the-Counter market?

A The basic source for any information on OTC stocks is the Standard & Poor's Reports. These are a collection of looseleaf sheets in ringed binders. (The separate volumes are available for all NYSE and AMEX companies.) These sheets are updated at least once a quarter and more frequently if developments warrant. Every brokerage house and many libraries have sets of these reports. Standard & Poor's and Moody's Investor Services both issue annual bound volumes, which can be found in many libraries.

If you wish to own your own complete directory, two are issued, annually and semiannually, by the National Association of Securities Dealers, the organization supervising brokers and the OTC markets. They are the NASDAQ Company Directory ($10), updated every six months; and the NASDAQ Fact Book and Company Directory ($15), which also includes complete reports on the previous year's OTC markets. Either volume is available from NASD, 1735 K Street NW, Washington, D.C. 20006-1506.

capital and surplus of $2 million;
minimum price per share of $3.00; and
two market makers

A majority of these companies are startups and spend most of their budgets on research and development; hence there are no set earnings requirements. To be included on the OTC Bulletin Board, a company's 100,000 publicly held shares must have a market value of $200,000.

The 1992 fee schedule for these stocks and the 4,000 pink-sheet stocks using the Bulletin Board includes a one-time initial entry payment of $5,000 and then up to $5,000 to cover each class of stock. The maximum annual NASD fee per issuer is $6,000.

(In a bid to attract more stock listings, in early 1992 the

American Stock Exchange introduced what it called "an Emerging Company Marketplace" as a competitive alternative to NASDAQ Small Cap listings. Under the AMEX scheme, a company needs a minimum of 250,000 shares held by no fewer than 300 public stockholders; a trading price of at least $1.00 per share if previously traded on NASDAQ or $3.00 per share if the stock is a new initial public offering (IPO); and a total market value of publicly and privately held shares of $2.5 million. The listing fee is $5,000. The AMEX Emerging Company Marketplace started with twenty-two listings on March 18 and within six months the trading lists, reported daily in *The Wall Street Journal*, totaled thirty companies. (One of the original companies, as the AMEX hoped would be the pattern, had increased in value and moved up to a regular AMEX listing.)

Many newspapers that can't afford to devote much space to OTC price quotations publish a shortened list, often labeled *Local OTC Stocks*, of companies in their circulation area. This list is provided by the local NASD office and may include stocks from all three of the listing systems.

It is evident that the NASD's three common-stock electronic computer services—the NASDAQ National Market System, the NASDAQ Small Cap Market, and the OTC Bulletin Board (including some pink-sheet quotes)—offer a more efficient, cheaper, and modern trading system than the traditional broker, specialist, and floor exchange transactions with attendant commissions at each of the three steps. Each trading system is energetically competing to survive, and no one can predict the outcome.

8

Mutual Funds

Now that you've gotten a good handle on reading common-stock quotation pages, it is time to decide how you should invest. There are two key variables to consider: the market volatility; and your short- or long-term strategy.

In earlier, less innovative days, when the trading volume was much lower, market trends were readily discernible. There were weeks of steady increases often followed by days of slow declines, then considered necessary corrections. Today, with large block institutional trading and instant dumping of entire multimillion-dollar portfolios in a single transaction for the purchase of futures in the same stocks (called *program trading*), steep market corrections occur daily, often in the last hour of trading. This volatility tends to scare smaller-sum investors and discourage individual common-stock buying.

There is no doubt that the stock market today is controlled by institutional investors—block trading by multibillion-dollar pension funds and insurance companies, investment bankers, and cash-laden mutual funds. A novice investor can't compete in this league. Until you become more savvy, it's better to join the herd and invest with mutual funds managed by professionals.

In 1981 there were 581 mutual funds with $123.7 billion of assets under management. Now there are more than 3,700 funds with assets in excess of $1.3 trillion (yes, trillion), according to the Investment Company Institute, the Washington, D.C., group that monitors and represents the fund industry.

That is remarkable growth, and what is more significant, nearly half those assets are invested in both taxable and tax-exempt money market mutual funds, money once deposited in sundry bank savings accounts earning lower interest.

So what is a mutual fund? It is the handiest way imaginable for smaller-sum investors to have their savings bundled into million-dollar portfolios managed by investment professionals who can buy stocks, bonds, and other income issues in large blocks. This is one way to avoid the volatile markets and compete with the program traders at less cost than individual purchases.

There are two types of mutual funds: the more popular are called *open-end* and the other, *closed-end*. Open-end funds can be issued by fund managers in unlimited numbers and can be bought or redeemed instantly at the current market price of the portfolio. Closed-end funds, like any common-stock issues, have a limited number of shares and trade on a stock exchange at whatever price anyone is willing to pay. (Closed-end funds are discussed separately in chapter 11.)

By law, no mutual fund is supposed to be sold until the investor has been given a prospectus of the fund by either the fund sponsors, who sell directly to the public, or the stock-

Q I've read about *socially responsible* mutual funds. What are they and where are they available?

A There are several such funds. The trouble is deciding what is socially responsible. No fund can meet every investor's yardstick. Some avoid munitions makers, others nuclear power producers, others environmental polluters, etc. So each investor must scan the portfolios and decide. Here are the six with the longest track records:

Calvert Social Investment Fund (800-368-2748) offers both a money fund and a growth-stock portfolio that "seek to provide an economic and social return to society that will contribute to the quality of life for all."

Dreyfus Third Century Fund (800-645-6561) "evaluates companies' performance in the areas of environmental protection...occupational health and safety...consumer protection...equal employment opportunity." (The fund does not exclude defense contractors or liquor producers.)

New Alternatives Fund (516-466-0808), while not founded as an ethical fund, concentrates on solar and alternative-energy companies.

Pax World Fund (603-431-8022) "endeavors to make a contribution to world peace through investments in companies producing life-supportive goods and services."

Pioneer Funds I, II, and III (617-742-7825). The original Pioneer Fund was founded in 1928 and is the oldest fund managing money along ethical lines, shunning investments in alcohol and tobacco. Two of the funds also exclude drug companies.

Parnassus Fund (415-664-6812) is not a socially responsible fund in the accepted sense but has five portfolio-selection criteria warranting its inclusion. Companies included are thought to have high-quality products and marketing-oriented management, be innovative and responsive to change, have a reputation for treating their employees well, and are considered sensitive to the surrounding communities.

brokers (and nowadays insurance agents), who sell a variety of funds issued by different sponsors.

The prospectus is required to outline such things as a fund's investment objective, how it can be purchased, and all attendant fees. This information is always phrased in stuffy protective legalese, as favored by the Securities and Exchange Commission, but there must be a summary page up front for us non-lawyers. Digest this page and you are ready to select a fund.

What kind of mutual fund should you select? A seemingly endless number of different funds are available, and the list grows weekly. The real answer depends on your investment goals, the degree of risk you are willing to assume, and your age. Here is my general yardstick for three investor age groups:

• A young investor with long-range goals and less need for income should consider an Aggressive Growth or Capital Appreciation stock fund, which often pays no dividend but has the potential for an increase in stock price (capital gain) over time.

• A middle-aged person with family responsibilities should perhaps select a Growth and Income fund (often called an Equity-Income fund), which combines capital gain with acceptable current dividend income.

• An older person, who may need dividend income, should think about bond and utility stock funds, or what are called Balanced funds—a combination of stocks and bonds.

Whatever their age, all investors should start structuring diversified portfolios—many experts recommend one-third stocks, one-third bonds, and one-third cash equivalents, such as money funds or Treasuries. The exact percentages needn't be frozen and can periodically be changed, as long as you don't have "all your eggs in one basket," and the value of your portfolio will keep pace with inflation.

To help you select funds that meet your goals, you need to have access to a good directory, rather than just scanning ads in the financial pages or magazines.

One of the best starter volumes is the *Guide to Mutual Funds*, published by the Investment Company Institute. The first fifteen pages of the *Guide* offer as comprehensible and complete an overview of mutual funds as any novice needs. The following 150-some pages are a directory of 3,726 funds listed by twenty-two categories of investment objectives. Each entry includes the fund address and a toll-free telephone number, the name of the investment adviser (sometimes different from the fund sponsor), total assets, minimum initial investment, and instructions on how to buy (either direct from the sponsor or through a broker). Nowhere else can you get such basic and necessary information for just $5.00. Write to Investment Company Institute, 1600 M St. NW, Washington, D.C. 20036.

Next you need a performance reference and information about a fund's fee schedule. One of the best available is the IBC/Donoghue's *Mutual Funds Almanac* ($34.95; IBC/Donoghue, Box 8008, Ashland, MA 01721-9104). In addition to the usual directory information, the *Almanac* details year-by-year returns and shows what $10,000 invested in each fund was worth over five- and ten-year periods through December 31 of the previous year. More importantly, three key expense figures, all affecting potential annual earnings, are given: sales and redemption charges; management's annual fees; and any extra annual fees that are deducted for marketing. (Such deductions are allowed up to 1.25 percent of assets under what is called a 12(b)1 plan.)

Granted this is a somewhat expensive investment tool, especially since you would want to check every year for current

> Q Is there any one time when it is better than others to buy mutual funds?
>
> A Each fund is required by law to distribute 95 percent of all earnings and capital gains each year to its fund holders. Most do so in December. Immediately after any distribution is announced, the net asset value of the fund shares drops by the same amount. If you bought shares just before the record date for these dividends, you would be incurring an added tax liability for that tax year. If you bought after the record date, you would get more shares for the same amount of money invested. Before buying any fund check on the earnings and capital-gain distribution dates.

figures and other changes. Before buying see if your local library has the *Almanac* or will add it to its business section.

Two less costly sources are the annual fund ratings issue of *Forbes* magazine, published in early September, and the *Barron's/Lipper Index*, published quarterly beginning in February.

The *Forbes* report offers a unique performance rating system for each fund in "Up" and "Down" stock markets, a ten-year and latest twelve-month total return (trading price per share as of June 30, plus dividends and any capital gains declared in the previous year), and its own computation of a fund's annual expenses per $100 invested.

The quarterly Lipper Analytical Services report of mutual fund performance, published in *Barron's* financial weekly, is timely, readily available, and reasonably priced ($2.50), not only for the Lipper charts but also for the many analytical articles on mutual fund doings. An informative and unique feature of this report is the separate fee costs for load, 12(b)1 plans, and redemptions.

More current Lipper mutual fund indexes are published regularly in the financial sections of many Sunday newspapers and magazines. Each day *The Wall Street Journal* on its mutual fund quotation page carries a Lipper-prepared chart of the *Top 15 Performers and the Bottom 10 Performers* in different fund investment categories. These charts cover total return figures for the previous month, the year to date, the past twelve months, and the past five years. If I were using these charts to help me pick a fund, or compare my present holdings, I'd rely solely on the twelve-month and the five-year figures. Anything shorter is just trying to outguess the market.

Once you have a handle on fund performance records, you need to start comparing investment fees.

Fund Fees

All funds charge an annual management fee. Half of 1 percent was once the accepted standard fee, with others varying up to 1 percent, the very highest. Now, according to Lipper, the average management fee for a stock fund is almost three-quarters of 1 percent, and many—especially those that change their portfolios frequently—are charging from 1 to 2 percent. These charges are deducted from assets in the portfolio regardless of whether the fund shares are up or down in price.

The more commonly known costs associated with mutual fund investing are the sales commissions, called *loads*. The basic categories are straightforward and readily identified.

No-load funds charge no up-front sales commission; you can buy from and sell shares back to the sponsor without any charge. You invest $5,000, or whatever initial minimum, and every cent is immediately invested in X number of shares.

Low-load funds charge any amount up to 4½ percent. For example, if you invest $5,000 in this type of fund, only $4,775 will be used to buy fund shares. The remaining $225 is the up-front 4½ percent load.

Full-load funds once charged a standard 8.5 percent (only $4,575 of the hypothetical sum would be used to buy the first shares) but most now collect from 5.5 to 6.5 percent.

With the exception of retirement accounts, dividends reinvested to buy more shares will also be subject to the same original load charge.

Many formerly full-load funds have introduced a new wrinkle to make them competitive with the no-loads. It is called a *contingent deferred sales charge.* There are no up-front commissions ($5,000 invested buys $5,000 of shares), but an investor redeeming shares within the first year of purchase typically would pay a 6 percent fee, which would be reduced by 1 percent a year until there would be no redemption penalty.

Loads and deferred sales fees are normally assessed to cover commissions paid to brokers or agents. Some fund sponsors also believe the fees discourage frequent traders or fund switchers.

There is no agreement about which funds—no-load, low-load, or full-load—will be the most profitable over time. There are historic instances of each category outperforming the other. My own inclination is to find and stick with the no-loads.

Reading the Daily Charts

When checking the daily mutual fund chart, it is easy to spot the different loads.

The boldface type identifies the sponsor. Under that heading, on a slightly indented line, are the separate funds managed by the same group. A lightface type entry without any indentation indicates an individual fund.

The first column of figures gives the fund's *net asset value* (NAV), the per-share value of stocks in the portfolio, which is figured daily after the markets close. This is the bid price—what you would pay per share if the fund were no-load, or what you would get if you redeemed shares of a load fund.

The next column is variously labeled *offer price* or *ask price*. The no-load funds have an *NL* in this column of figures (you can either buy or sell at the same price). The other funds show a higher price than the NAV in this column; the difference is the load charge. The final column, labeled NAV Chg, shows the net change in cents and dollars from the previous day's quotations.

The daily mutual fund charts also include some very important lowercase letters that can help you evaluate a fund:

e—The shares traded that day are *ex-dividend*, meaning that the buyer will not get a recently declared dividend. In effect, the buyer becomes responsible for the amount of the dividend for income tax purposes and five business days later (the permissible settlement period for any trades) will own a share reduced in value by the same amount as the dividend

f—The price quotations are from the previous day's trading because the fund sponsor failed to report to the National Association of Securities Dealers, which compiles and distributes these daily figures through the financial wire services

s—The stock has recently been split or a dividend has been declared

CHART 8

Mutual Funds

The daily mutual fund chart shows trading prices for all mutual funds with at least 1,000 shareholders or $25 million in assets. These are the "open-end" funds, simply meaning that there is no set number of shares outstanding, and more shares are issued as demand warrants. The encircled examples show:

1—Evergreen Funds in boldface type identifies the management company (Evergreen Asset Management of Purchase, N.Y.), and the six following name abbreviations are the separate funds. They are: Evergreen, all common stocks; the Foundation, a combined stock and bond fund; Limited Market, small company growth fund; Municipal, tax-exempt bonds; American Retirement Trust, another balanced fund of common stocks and bonds; Total Return, stocks combining steady dividends and capital gains; and Value Timing, capital appreciation with frequent trading and portfolio turnover. All seven of these funds are no-load (you can buy or sell at the same price given in the first column). The "NL" in the next column confirms this. The last column shows plus or minus cents based on the valuation of the stocks in the fund portfolio at the close of the last trading day.

2—The next entry, "ExcelMID," stands for Excel Midas Gold Shares, an entirely different fund managed by Excel Advisers of San Diego. This fund has an up-front load charge of 4½ percent. To buy a share on this day cost $2.58. If you had sold, you would have received only $2.46.

	Evergreen Funds:			
	Evgrn	12.82	NL	+.03
	Found	11.27	NL	+.02
	LtdMk	19.36	NL	+.01
❶	MunIF	2.05	NL	...
	Retire	10.77	NL	...
	TotRtn	19.07	NL	...
	ValTm	12.88	NL	−.02
	ExcelMid	2.46	2.58	−.01
	ExcHY p	7.42	7.79	...
❷	FAM Val	17.92	17.92	+.06
	FBL BIC	16.17	16.17	−.01

Chart reproduced with permission from the Associated Press.

p—The fund has a 12(b)1 distribution and marketing charge

r—The fund charges a redemption fee

t—The fund has both a 12(b)1 and a redemption charge.

These letters give you an idea as to whether you want to research a fund further, without even consulting a fund directory.

During the first year or two of mutual fund investing, make sure that the fund sponsor regularly sends you the "Statement of Additional Information," which includes a list of all the stocks, bonds, or cash equivalents in the portfolio. Some funds send this annually, others quarterly. By checking previous issues you can determine what stocks your fund experts bought or sold. Now, perhaps, you are ready to try your own hand at single-stock investing.

9

Picking Common Stocks

There is no foolproof formula for successful investing in common stocks. Even the professionals have their share of winners and losers. You, too, will have your share. Since this is your first venture, buy stocks of high-quality companies and follow the age-based selection formula mentioned for buying mutual fund shares in the previous chapter.

For the young aggressive investor, now is an ideal time to buy shares of biotechnology companies, most of which don't pay any dividends but are certainly the profitable stocks of tomorrow. Alternatively, consider computer mainframe, software, CAD-CAM imaging, and artificial intelligence companies, many of which have been battered by reduced domestic demand but still have great earnings potential as the U.S. economy recovers and vast overseas markets blossom. Buy stocks in both these groups in down markets.

The middle-aged investor should concentrate on stock purchases of established companies with good dividend-paying track records, such as du Pont, IBM, Ford, General Motors, any one of many pharmaceutical companies, and consumer-product giants such as Kellogg's, Coca-Cola, and Gillette. Not only will these companies provide needed dividend income, they will also have above-average potential for capital gain.

The older investor with income foremost in mind should have a sampling of telephone and utility stocks, both for their regular dividends and their potential for capital gain. The utilities should be selected not only by comparing price and dividend yield but also with some idea of the source of power—oil, coal, nuclear, or hydro—and the regulatory climate of the states served. Until there is a change in the national attitude toward nuclear power facilities, it is a good idea to avoid those utilities relying on nuclear power generation. Good sources for such information are *Value Line Investment Survey*, available in any brokerage office and many banks and libraries, and the *United & Babson Investment Report*, which is published weekly. (The annual subscription fee is $215; for a free introductory sample, write to United & Babson, 101 Prescott Street, Wellesley Hills, MA 02181.) United & Babson annually updates its list of major utilities with a breakdown of the percentages of fuels used.

In the long term all three stock portfolios should be diversified by whatever mix of industries suits your fancy. Remember, good times or bad, the successful providers of food, drugs, transportation, and utilities will be in business and will be profitable. Once the core of your portfolio is in high-quality stocks, arbitrarily designate a specific smaller sum for regular investments in other, less-essential, industries, or even some long shots.

Many in the investment business caution against falling in

Q I own stocks of established companies trading on the NYSE and NASDAQ that are held in *street name* by the brokers. Are brokers required to forward company quarterly reports to me?

A According to a Securities and Exchange commission official, SEC Code 14b-1, Obligations of a Broker, Paragraph B, says that upon receipt of proxy forms and annual reports, the broker must forward them promptly to the owners of stock held in a street-name account. He says there is no specific obligation concerning interim (or quarterly) reports. A NASDAQ spokesman says its listed companies and member brokers are required to distribute directly or through a broker annual reports and proxy material in a timely manner before an annual meeting. Any interim or quarterly reports merely have to be made available upon request. Actually, there is no reason why a broker should not comply with these rules. The issuing companies provide the documents and pay the broker a fee and the cost of mailing.

Q When reading proxy statements I sometimes note a reference to checking a box if I wish to attend the annual meeting, but there never is a card enclosed. Don't street-name stockholders ever get these cards?

A No. The corporation has no idea who owns the stock. Your shares are among hundreds, perhaps thousands, of shares held by the brokerage house. Under new SEC regulations the names of people with street-name accounts must be provided to a corporation, with the individuals' permission. It is assumed, though, that corporations will seek this list only when there is a critical vote pending, such as a takeover attempt.

love with your stock picks. That's good advice for a trader, but I would rather see smaller-sum investors buy high-quality stocks and hold them long term: no less than five years and, preferably, ten or more years. Learn to ignore the up-and-down price fluctuations; in time your stocks will be worth substantially more than your purchase price.

When possible buy shares in round lots (one hundred shares per lot). The commissions will be lower, and they will be more readily salable at a specific price. In the case of a higher-priced stock, such as IBM or most of the drug stocks, buy an even number of fewer shares until you have a round lot in your portfolio.

Do you need a broker? The answer to that question can be found by reading the daily or weekly financial press or watching any television show specializing in investments. Time after time the experts are trotted out and offer conflicting advice. Who's right, and when? The truth is you could be right just as often as the "experts."

Many novice investors seem to forget that there are thousands of brokers just trying to make a week's wage. They don't particularly care whether the market is up or down as long as they generate commissions. Very few smaller-sum investors get alerted to a genuine stock-buying opportunity by a broker.

So unless you want a broker to hold your hand and jingle your phone regularly, make your own decisions and open a self-directed account with a discount broker. You won't get any advice or be persuaded to invest in something unsuitable, but you will be buying stocks for considerably lower commissions. (See chapter 15 for a rundown of the unique assistance a full-service brokerage does offer.)

Another Way to Build a Portfolio

There are at least 1,000 major corporations that will issue additional shares to stockholders instead of paying cash dividends. These are called *dividend reinvestment plans* (DRIPs), and most such plans permit optional cash purchases per month, per quarter, or per year of substantial sums to buy more shares, often without cost and even at a small discount to current market price per share.

This, of course, means you must first be a stockholder and sign up for the DRIPs. Some corporations say one share is all you need to start; a very few will sell the first shares directly to you. Nine such are American Recreation Centers, Central Vermont Public Service, Chemical Bank Corp (recently merged with Manufacturers Hanover), Citicorp, Exxon, W. R. Grace, Great Northern Nekoosa, Johnson Controls, and Kroger Co.

To find out which corporations offer DRIPs, check the S&P Stock Report sheets, call a company you may be interested in, or obtain the *Directory of Companies Offering Reinvestment Plans* published by Evergreen Enterprises ($19.95: write to Evergreen Enterprises, P.O. Box 763, Laurel, MD 20725). This volume gives specifics on cost, discount, and amounts of permissible optional cash purchases.

There are at least two other ways to get your first shares without paying excessive brokerages fees. Join the National Association of Investment Clubs (1515 East Eleven Mile Road, Royal Oak, MI 48067), or become a subscriber to the investment newsletter *Moneypaper* ($63 annually; 1010 Mamaroneck Avenue, Mamaroneck, NY 10543). NAIC members can buy single shares of stock through the parent organization, and the newsletter lists about twenty different stocks each month that can be bought through the publisher for the current market price plus a $15.00 fee.

Investors with stocks held in street name at a brokerage house cannot elect to have dividends reinvested nor make any optional cash purchases.

10

Bonds

Investing in bonds is probably the trickiest of all investment strategies, and with few very exceptions bond buying is best left to bond brokers or mutual fund managers. There are many reasons for this.

First and foremost, unless bonds are held to maturity (something often beyond an investor's control), the value of your original investment can change daily—and sometimes precipitously.

Second, there is an almost endless variety of bonds available, each requiring some specialized knowledge.

Third, there is limited public reporting on a daily basis in the financial press, so it is not easy on any given day to know the value of your holdings.

Fourth, all bonds have a known maturity date, but most have early call dates, and these are the key to what you will actually be earning in interest. A bond that sounds, at the time of issue, as if it will be earning 9 percent may actually turn out to yield significantly lower returns if it is redeemed early and the only substitute bonds available for reinvestment of the principal now are paying only, say, 7 percent.

What is a bond? It is a certificate representing a loan by an investor to any number of legal entities (federal, state, city, or corporate) earning a set annual interest rate and with a stated maturity date, or provisions (often not emphasized) for early call dates when you will be paid off at the par or face value of the bond.

Bonds were once issued in $1,000 increments and had interest coupons attached, which were clipped on payment days and processed through a bank. Some of these so-called *bearer bonds* are still outstanding. Nowadays bonds are usually issued in $5,000 increments and are registered with the issuer's agent in an investor's name. Interest payments are sent directly to the investor or his or her broker.

Bonds are rated according to the risk an investor is taking with regard to the issuer's likelihood of repaying the loan. The two major rating companies are Standard & Poor's and Moody's Investors Service. Both use letter symbols, with Triple A (*AAA* for S & P and *Aaa* for Moody's) representing the highest-quality rating; Double A (*AA* or *Aa*) designating high quality but not as good as the top rating; Single A considered to have sound capacity to repay; and Triple B (*BBB* for S&P and *Baa* for Moody's) regarded as having adequate repayment capacity, subject to economic conditions or changing circumstances.

Only bonds carrying these top ratings are said to be of *investment grade*, which simply means that certain trustees, pension funds, and mutual funds can buy only bonds in these categories. Other mutual funds and private investors are, of course, free to take greater risks and seek higher yields from bonds rated below investment grade.

Q Where would a municipal bond issued by a hospital fit in a range of excellent to poor? The bond is rated BBB and Baa1. What do all those letters and the number 1 mean?

A If this hospital is located in a thriving community, its bonds would be a safe investment. The letters and number are the separate ratings given the bond issue by Standard & Poor's and Moody's Investor Services, the two most frequently used municipal bond raters. Here are the specific definitions for each rating:

Standard & Poor's

AAA—Highest rating, with an extremely strong capacity to pay interest and repay principal.

AA—Differ from the highest-rated bonds in only a small degree.

A—A strong capacity to pay interest and repay principal, but somewhat susceptible to any changes in economic conditions.

BBB—Regarded as having an adequate capacity to pay interest and repay principal.

All lower S&P ratings are thought to have varying speculative elements.

Moody's Investor Services

Aaa—The best quality with the smallest degree of investment risk.

Aa—Judged to be of high quality by all standards.

A—Considered upper-medium grade obligations with adequate security as to principal and interest.

Baa—Considered medium-grade obligations, neither highly protected nor poorly secured. The number 1 after the letter grade indicates that the bonds have maximum security within their quality group.

All lower Moody's ratings are judged to have varying degrees of speculative elements.

The lower ratings, all believed to be speculative investments with descending prospects of ever repaying the loans, are *BB* for S&P, *Ba* for Moody's; single B for both; *CCC* for S&P and *Caa* for Moody's; *CC* for S&P and *Ca* for Moody's; C for both; and D for S&P. All of the C ratings denote bonds that are in default. In each category a plus or minus sign may appear after the letters, which indicates slight positive or negative variations from most other bonds in the same category.

All Treasury securities (bonds, notes, and bills) are unrated, for the obvious reason that they carry the "full faith and credit" of the U.S. government. If the government defaults, everything else is in trouble. (Treasuries were discussed in detail in chapter 1.) Here are some of the other bonds.

The best known bonds are called *municipals* (or *munis*, for short), and the interest earnings are usually exempt from federal tax. Two exceptions to federal tax exemption are that the bond earnings for taxpayers in certain brackets are added to total adjusted gross earnings for possible assessment of the alternate minimum tax, and some state industrial development bonds (described below) are now subject to a state-by-state quota. Interest on any bonds sold in excess of that quota are considered taxable income by the Internal Revenue Service.

In most cases investors living in the same state as the issuing entity will not pay any state tax on these earnings; hence they are called *double tax-exempts*. There also are *triple tax-exempts* for residents of New York City and Philadelphia, which levy a separate city income tax.

The term *municipal* covers a vast array of debt offerings. The major ones are a state's, a city's, or a town's general obligation bonds, with the money being used for schools, roads, etc., and the bond interest paid out of citizen taxes; revenue bonds for a specific project, such as a toll road or sewer line, for which the ultimate user (home owner or motorist-trucker) will be charged a fee, providing the issuing authority with a revenue stream to pay the bondholders; and industrial development bonds, with the proceeds possibly benefiting a private company, such as a utility plant serving the public, a manufacturing plant installing pollution-control equipment, a new factory creating local jobs, or a hotel-motel as part of a city's urban redevelopment project. Depending on a state's quota, bonds for the latter category may or may not be considered exempt from federal tax.

Most of these bonds are sold in minimum increments of $5,000 and, as mentioned earlier, transactions are more efficiently handled by a bond brokerage, which can allot interest payments on the due date to each client's account and monitor for any early call dates. The one exception is if you live in a state's capital city, where the major commercial banks have a municipal bond department. Such banks invariably are lead underwriters for local issues and publish a weekly sheet of bonds available. If you can conveniently visit such a bank department, these bonds can be bought and serviced easily without a broker. The per-bond offering price paid either to an underwriting bank or a broker includes the commission, normally about 3 percent.

An alternative method for this type of tax-exempt investment is the *unit investment trust* (UIT), available through brokers, which is a bundling of several tax-exempt bond issues with approximately similar maturity dates. When a UIT is issued, a fixed interest rate for the entire portfolio is set, and the investor usually can elect to receive interest payments monthly, quarterly, or semiannually, with the longer payment intervals earning fractionally more.

In theory, by the time all issues in the UIT portfolio ma-

> Q A good deal of my assets are in municipal bonds held in two
> brokerage accounts. Short of the state or city defaulting, is
> there any way I can lose if the brokers went bankrupt?
>
> A Your holdings are perfectly safe. All holdings in a major bro-
> kerage account are independently insured for no less than
> $500,000 by the Securities Investor Protection Corp. (SIPC), a fed-
> eral government–chartered but industry-financed and -operated in-
> surer. Normally, when a brokerage bankruptcy occurs, the actual
> street-name holdings of clients' stocks and bonds are automatically
> transferred to a solvent broker, and the SIPC assumes responsibility
> for up to $100,000 of any cash balance credited to the account.

ture, the par value of the units will be paid to the investor. In
practice, some of the bonds may be paid off earlier, and the
regular checks will include both interest and return of principal. If an investor fails to monitor and reinvest any return of
principal, both the periodic interest payments and the value
of the unit will be lower.

Whether buying individual municipals, unit investment
trusts, or a bond mutual fund, an investor can protect the
bonds from default by selecting an insured issue. With so
much talk about state and city financial trouble and taxpayer
resistance to higher levies, many bond issuers have been insuring the issue for payment of today's trading price (not maturity par) and accumulated interest at the time of any default.
This costs about one-half of 1 percent in interest earnings
and most frequently is covered by such insurers as MBIA
(Municipal Bond Investors Assurance Corp.), AMBAC Indemnity Corp. (originally American Municipal Bond Assurance Corp., co-owned by Citicorp, now a public stock
company), or FGIC (Financial Guarantee Insurance Co., a

General Electric Corp. subsidiary). For about the same fee, large international banks have also been issuing letters of credit to bond sponsors, thus improving the creditworthiness of these issues. All bonds with either backing have automatically been given Triple A ratings. This cuts the interest cost to the issuer (in a sense offsetting the premiums and fees paid to the guarantors) and also permits purchase of the bonds by those restricted to investment-grade issues.

Corporate bonds and other interest-paying debt issues are second only to common and preferred stocks for a corporation's long-term financing and short-term cash needs. Unlike municipals the fixed-interest payments are fully taxable to an investor by both the federal and state governments, but the rate of return is higher, and a bond buyer is a protected creditor, depending on what issues are bought. The variety is endless, starting with regular bonds trading publicly through stock exchanges.

Then there are countless bond-type issues sold directly to investment bankers and national brokerage houses to be resold in large blocks and rarely available to smaller-sum investors. These secondary issues include

- *convertible bonds,* which can be used later to acquire common stock, often at a preferential price similar to preferred stocks;
- *short-term corporate notes* issued by such customer financing giants as GMAC, Ford, Chrysler, and commercial banks, backed by car buyer or credit-card payments and usually paying an investor fractionally more than Treasury securities with the same maturities;
- *equipment leasing bonds,* favored by railroads and airlines and backed by corporate rental payments;
- *debentures, subordinated notes,* and *senior notes,* many with no

collateral or limited to the creditworthiness of the issuer;
- *zero-coupon bonds*, which can be bought at a fraction of maturity value but pay no interest and incur a computed annual tax liability;
- and last, but far from least during the high-flying corporate buyouts of the 1980s, *junk bonds* (also called *high-yield bonds*), invariably issued with enticing interest rates, unpredictable risks, and uncertain maturity dates.

Few of these secondary bond investments belong in the portfolio of a novice investor, while any or all could be profitable investments in shares of a professionally managed mutual fund with a portfolio of many separate issues with minimal risk of total loss.

Government bonds should be ranked at the top of every novice investor's "stop and look" list, largely because mutual funds have loosely used the term *government* in fund names and advertising, hoping to lure investors who may unwittingly assume this means a risk-free investment. The only government issues without any risk are U.S. Treasury securities (see chapter 1). All the other so-called government bonds are issued by numerous agencies created by Congress but are not necessarily guaranteed by the present or future Congresses. All are subject to the same market and fluctuating interest rates that affect common stocks and bonds, money market funds, and bank certificates of deposit.

This does not mean that government-agency bonds are not a good and reasonably safe investment. Most pay fractionally higher interest than comparable Treasury securities, but the principal invested will have wide swings during the life of the issue.

There are many government-agency bonds, most with earnings subject to federal and state income tax and only one, a Ginnie Mae (Government National Mortgage Association), with principal and current interest guaranteed by the U.S. government. Ginnie Maes, available singly at $25,000 or in a mutual fund, generally earn fractionally more or about the same interest as the current prime lending rate. Two other bond issues representing a bundling of home mortgages subsidized by the federal government and earning about the same interest as Ginnie Maes are Fannie Maes (Federal National Mortgage Association) and Freddie Macs (Federal Home Loan Mortgage Corporation).

There is a whole slew of similar agency bonds. A short list would include Student Loan Marketing Association, Federal Farm Credit Banks, Tennessee Valley Authority, World Bank, and Inter-American Development Bank. All can be bought as original issues or most often at less-cost through a very active secondary market handled by a broker. The terms run from a few months to many years.

At the beginning of this chapter, it was suggested that it is better, especially for a novice, to invest in bonds through a specialist broker or a mutual fund. I hope you have a better idea now why that's sound advice.

CHART 10

Corporate Bonds

Few bonds are listed and traded on the stock exchanges. Most are bought and sold through dealer-to-dealer transactions reported daily on the "yellow sheets," compiled and distributed to brokers by the National Quotations Bureau, or by professional bond traders through direct electronic communications. The limited trading quotations seen in the daily financial press are for corporate bonds. The accompanying chart shows:

1—AMR, an abbreviation for the issuer (the holding company for American Airlines), the stated interest rate of 9 percent—the "s" merely separates the numbers—and 16, the year 2016 when the bond matures.

2—Current Yield of 8.9 percent, based on the price above 100 of the last trade.

3—Volume: Unlike stock quotations, this number is the total value in thousands of dollars of the day's trading; in this case $207,000 worth of bonds traded.

4—Close, the price for the last trade per $1,000 bond, or $1,015, to earn 8.9 percent, not the 9 percent par value.

5—Net Change (minus 3/8ths) from the previous day's trade.

❶	❷	❸	❹	❺
	Cur			Net
Bonds	Yld	Vol	Close	Chg.
AMR 9s16	8.9	207	101 ½	− ⅜
AMR zr06	...	50	43 ½	+ ¼
Advst 9s08	cv	61	90	+ ½
AirbF 6¾01	cv	20	87 ¼	...
AlaP 7⅞s02	7.7	3	102	...
AlskAr 6⅞14	cv	25	81 ¾	− ¼
AlskAr zr06	...	60	34 ½	− ¼
Albnylnt 5s02	cv	45	79 ½	− ½
AlldC zr92	...	16	99⁵⁄₃₂	...
AlldC zr96	...	129	82 ¼	+ ¼
AlldC zr2000	...	15	55	− 1⅞
AlldC zr9	...	50	95⁹⁄₃₂	− ⁷⁄₃₂
AlldC zr95	...	45	85 ½	+ ¾
AlldC zr97	...	20	72 ⅝	+ 1⅞
AlldC zr99	...	60	61	− 1
AlldC zr01	...	5	49	− 1½

Chart reproduced with permission from the Associated Press.

11

Closed-end and Country Funds

S prinkled among the daily stock exchange quotations are scores of listings and trading prices for closed-end funds. Many of these are invested in common stocks of numerous foreign companies and hence are often referred to as *country funds*.

They are, in fact, the same as other mutual funds with one big difference: At the time of issue, only a specific number of shares are sold, rather than unlimited shares, as investors demand the better-known *open-end funds*. The sponsor of a closed-end fund, either a mutual fund group or a brokerage house, sells the known number just as any other initial public offering (IPO) of common stocks. If 1 million shares of a closed-end fund are sold at $10.00 each, the sponsor pockets the $10 million and invests in the common stock of companies in Thailand, Great Britain, or wherever he or she chooses.

Since investors cannot redeem the shares, the fund manager need not maintain a cash reserve and can keep the fund fully invested. In fact, once the fund issue is sold out, the sponsor has no further role except to hunt for profitable investments and disburse the earnings.

Even though the funds went public, or originally sold, at $10.00 per share, most are now trading at a very different price. If lower, it is at a *discount;* if higher, at a *premium,* from the offering price. In other words, the market decides what a share is worth on any given day, just as it does for any corporate stock, and an investor can sell or buy at that price. And just as with any stock purchase, the investor pays a brokerage commission for closed-end-fund transactions.

Most of the closed-end stock funds are listed and trade on the New York Stock Exchange, with a few others on the American Exchange and the NASDAQ. Details on the country, the region of the world, and each portfolio are included in Standard & Poor's publications, which are available in some libraries and all brokerage houses.

The daily stock-quotation pages for each exchange include trading ranges for the funds. *The Wall Street Journal* and *Barron's* also publish separate lists showing the exchange on which the fund is traded, the net asset value of the underlying portfolio, the week's closing price, and the plus or minus difference to the net asset value of the portfolio.

During the 1990s most country funds have traded at a discount, some very substantially, largely because of a weaker U.S. dollar and, in some cases, uncertain economic conditions abroad. Some saw this as an opportunity to buy, and there is no doubt that these funds will prove to be good investments in the long term, especially if they are not purchased at the first offering price, which always includes substantial commissions to the underwriting brokers or mutual fund sponsors.

In addition to the many country funds, there are other closed-end funds that invest only in U.S. common stocks and

Q I own shares of the Mexico Fund, traded on the NYSE. A small portion of the portfolio consists of one-month and three-month Mexican Treasury bills (Certificados de Tesoreria). A bank of Mexico report shows that these bills are yielding a staggering interest rate. Is this a reasonably safe investment? If so, how may a U.S. citizen purchase Mexican treasuries?

A An officer at the Washington office of Mexico's development bank, *Nationale Financiera*, says there are no restrictions on such investments by U.S. citizens. But, he adds, all such investments must be made through intermediary trusts, run by any number of New York branches of Mexican commercial banks or brokerage houses. Similarly, U.S. citizens can invest in stocks of Mexican companies. All earnings are subject to a 10 percent withholding tax and, of course, the inevitable wide swings in peso-to-dollar exchange rates.

Q My broker says he has newly issued shares of a closed-end fund. Should I invest?

A Never invest in the initial offering of a closed-end fund, whether a country fund or a domestic stock fund. The initial price includes the underwriters' commission and the fund shares are invariably trading at less than the first offering price within days. If you look at the trading chart for these closed-end stocks, you will note than many are trading at a discount to the underlying portfolios. So hold off until the market for this type of shares settles. Even the so-called hot issues tend to trade lower in a short time.

an even larger number specializing in bonds, convertible bonds, international bonds, and U.S. municipal bonds. In each case the fund sponsors and managers feel they can produce better returns by having a limited number of shares outstanding, without worrying about having sufficient cash reserves on hand to meet redemptions. Quotes on these

CHART 11

Closed-End Funds

These are the same chart samples displayed with chapters 5 and 6, but instead of highlighting common and preferred stocks, these encircled names and quotations are all for closed-end mutual funds. Like any stock issue, closed-end funds have a specific number of shares outstanding and must meet exchange listing and financial reporting requirements.

1— The six funds highlighted here are underwritten and managed by the Alliance Capital Management Corp. of New York, hence the "ACM" in each name. They are

ACM Government Income Fund;

ACM Government Opportunity Fund;

ACM Government Securities Fund;

ACM Government Spectrum Fund;

ACM Managed Income Fund;

ACM Managed Multi-Market Trust.

The first five funds normally have two-thirds or more treasury and government agencies bonds in the portfolios, with the remainder spread between corporate and foreign debt and cash. The Managed Multi-Market Trust essentially is a currency-hedging portfolio with bonds of some dozen countries, including the new European Economic Community currency units.

2— Elsewhere throughout the NYSE, NASDAQ, and AMEX stock tables you find listings and quotations for the so-called "country funds." For example, see the encircled "EuropeFD," which invests entirely in European countries. It was sponsored and is managed by Warburg Investment Management International (Jersey) Ltd. Note on this day fund shares traded for $11.75.

3— This chart appears Monday in *The Wall Street Journal* under the headline "Publicly Traded Funds." It indicates the exchange where the fund shares trade, the net assest value ($13.28) of all the shares in the portfolio as of that date, the previous Friday's trading price, and the percentage difference (minus 11.52 percent) from the value of the portfolio. Most such funds trade at a discount to the portfolio value, a few at a premium.

		52 Weeks Hi	Lo	Stock	Sym	Div	Yld %	PE	Vol 100s	Hi	Lo	Close	Net Chg
				-A-A-A-									
		16⅞	10⅝	AAR	AIR	.48	3.7	16	106	13	12⅞	12⅞	– ⅛
		11⅝	**10⅛**	**ACM Gvt Fc**	**ACG**	**.96**	**8.6**	**...**	**815**	**11⅛**	**11**	**11⅛**	**...**
		10⅜	**8⅞**	**ACM OppFd**	**AOF**	**.80**	**8.3**	**...**	**187**	**9**	**9½**	**9⅝**	**...**
		11¼	**9**	**ACM SecFd**	**GSF**	**.96**	**8.7**	**...**	**2928**	**11**	**10¾**	**11**	**+ ⅛**
❶		**9½**	**8**	**ACM SpctmFd**	**SI**	**.79**	**8.7**	**...**	**526**	**9⅛**	**8⅞**	**9⅛**	**+1⅛**
		9⅝	**8**	**ACM MgdIncFd**	**AMF**	**.95**	**10.0**	**...**	**897**	**9⅝**	**9**	**9½**	**...**
		12⅞	**10⅝**	**ACM MgdMultFd**	**MMF**	**1.08**	**9.4**	**...**	**79**	**11¾**	**11½**	**11½**	**– ⅛**
		2½	1	ADT wt			...	...	1175	2	1¾	1⅞	+ ⅛
	n	9½	5	ADT	ADT		...	...	9315	8¾	8	8¾	+
		32⅞	20¼	AFLAC	AFL	.44	1.5	16	746	30	29¾	30⅛	+
		26	15	AL LabsA	BMD	.18	.8	93	101	23⅛	23	23⅛	– ⅛
		2⅛	¾	AM Int	AM		...	...	134	1	15/16	15/16	– 1/16
		8¾	5¼	EscoElec	ESE		...	...	441	7	6⅞	7	...
		17⅜	7¾	Esterline	ESL			...	9	176	8⅝	8⅜	– ¼
		29¾	22¼	EthylCp	EY	.60	2.3	14	848	26½	26⅛	26½	+ ⅛
❷		**12½**	**10**	**EuropeFd**	**EF**	**1.74e**	**14.8**	**...**	**105**	**11¾**	**11⅝**	**11¾**	**+ ⅛**
		7⅜	5¼	EuroWtFd	EWF	.44e	6.6	...	65	6¾	6⅝	6⅝	+ ⅛
		18⅝	16⅝	Excelsior	EIS	1.44e	7.9	...	61	18¼	18	18¼	...
	n	40¼	27⅜	Exel	XL	1.13e	3.2	7	62	35	34¾	35	+ ⅜

	Fund Name	Stock Exch.	N.A. Value	Stock Price	% Diff.
	Emerging Mark Tele Fd	NYSE	13.83	15	+ 8.46
	Emerging Mexico Fd	NYSE	b19.95	16½	– 17.29
	Engex	AMEX	10.24	8⅝	– 15.77
❸	**Europe Fund**	**NYSE**	**13.28**	**11¾**	**– 11.52**
	1stAustraila	AMEX	10.46	9⅛	– 12.76
	First Financial Fund	NYSE	11.69	10½	– 10.18
	First Iberian	AMEX	9.39	7¾	– 17.47

Chart reproduced with permission from the Associated Press and the Investment Company Institute, Washington, D.C.

trades can also be found alphabetically in the regular stock market tables, or separately in *Barron's* or *The Wall Street Journal.*

The *Journal* and *Barron's* also publish trading quotes of most active stocks trading on Canadian and numerous overseas exchanges. These are markets for professionals only. There are too many unknowns associated with foreign stock buying, such as markets not regulated or managed as efficiently as U.S. markets, varying and irregular financial reporting customs, tax withholding on dividends (which may or may not be offset on U.S. returns), and the inevitable and always erratic foreign currency exchanging.

If you want to invest overseas, the preferable choices are the closed-end or open-end mutual funds. Many fund managers—such as Putnam, Scudder, and Templeton—have been trading overseas for decades and have specialists trained in the intricacies of foreign markets and currency transactions.

12

Indexes

S tatistics are the meat and potatoes of stock market reporting and diverse investing theories—the "can't-fail" evidence for some market timers of when to buy or sell. The novice investor with long-term goals need not spend too much time understanding these figures but should be sufficiently familiar with statistical indexes to know what is being written or talked about.

The Dow Jones Industrial Average

The granddaddy of all indexes is the Dow Jones Industrial Average (DJIA), the single number (up or down) reported every day in newspapers and on the evening television news.

This first stock-price index began in 1884 as a "Customer's Afternoon Letter" covering trading in eleven stocks, nine of which were railroads. The letter was compiled and distributed by Charles Henry Dow, who, with his partner,

Edward D. Jones, later founded Dow Jones & Co. and in 1889 started publishing *The Wall Street Journal*. By 1928 the Dow Average had grown to twenty stocks of the nation's biggest manufacturing companies. That year the list was expanded to thirty companies, the same number as today.

The present Dow Jones averages have four components: the industrial average of thirty diverse companies and industries; the transportation average of twenty airline, trucking, and freight companies; the utilities average of fifteen companies providing electricity, gas, and gas transmission; and the composite average of all sixty-five stocks. Except for certain market specialists, the most visible of these is the thirty-stock DJIA.

Over the years the list of thirty has changed very infrequently; any changes that have occurred have been the result of mergers, buyouts, and, more recently, increased concentration of the national economy on service industries.

In 1991 there were three substitutions. Navistar, the old farm-equipment manufacturer, was replaced by Caterpillar Inc., the heavy-construction equipment maker; USX Corp., now both a steel and oil company, was dropped in favor of Walt Disney Co., the first entertainment representative in the average; and, last, Primerica, the old American Can Co. and now an insurance and financial services conglomerate, was replaced by the investment banker J. P. Morgan & Co. Inc.

It used to be very simple to figure the DJIA. One simply added the closing prices of each stock and divided by eleven, the number of stocks represented, to get the average for that day's trading. But over the years, as more companies were added and substituted, and those companies split the total number of outstanding shares, it was necessary to change the divisor. In mid-June 1991, for example, after three recent substitutions, the divisor number was 0.559. The ever-changing

Q If, as you've said, the Dow Jones Industrial Average (DJIA) is a limited reflection of the day's stock-market trading, why is it the only one regularly quoted by most persons reporting financial news?

A Since it is the oldest index continuously in use, it has become the pyschologically popular yardstick and thus is a readily understood flag for the less-knowledgeable public. The professionals, who look for a wider yardstick on the day's market, almost universally follow the S&P 500 Index, or, if they are more interested in smaller capitalized stocks, the NASDAQ Composite, which far outdistanced the Dow Jones in 1991 trading and profitablility. Even Dow Jones Co. has begun to recognize the limited use of the DJIA and has itself just started what it calls the Dow Jones Equity Market Index, covering today's more extensive stock listings. But even this new index uses only what they call *primary-market* (their code words for the NYSE) prices.

number is published, daily as a footnote to the Dow Jones Averages chart in *The Wall Street Journal* or weekly in the Market Laboratory in *Barron's*.

If you are interested, you can figure the DJIA for yourself. Add the closing prices of all thirty stocks and then divide that sum by the current divisor. Your total will probably be fractionally different from the one published, because for some unexplained reason the *Journal* uses only the closing prices of trades on the NYSE (or what some unrealistic financial purists call the "primary" market) to compute the DJIA and ignores fractionally different prices of trades that may have occurred in any of the regional exchanges.

(Paradoxically, the NYSE closing-price charts in the newspapers use "composite" closing-price figures—including any different prices from regional exchanges, such as the Pacific

Stock Exchange, which has always continued trading for half an hour after trading ends in New York.)

Here are the thirty companies in the Dow Jones Industrial Average:

Allied Signal Inc.
Aluminum Company of American (Alcoa)
American Express Co.
American Telephone & Telegraph Co.
Bethlehem Steel Corp.
Boeing Corp.
Caterpillar Inc.
Chevron Corp.
Coca-Cola Co.
Walt Disney Co.
E. I. du Pont de Nemours & Co.
Eastman Kodak Co.
Exxon Corp.
General Electric Co.
General Motors Corp.
Goodyear Tire & Rubber Co.
International Business Machines Corp.
International Paper Co.
McDonald's Corp.
Merck & Co.
Minnesota Mining & Manufacturing Co. (3M)
J. P. Morgan & Co. Inc.
Philip Morris Cos. Inc.
Procter & Gamble Co.
Sears, Roebuck & Co.
Texaco Inc.
Union Carbide Corp.

United Technologies Corp. (Pratt & Whitney and Sikorsky)
Westinghouse Electric Corp.
Woolworth Corp.

A quick glance shows that the index is both over- and underrepresentative of today's American industry and economy. For instance, Chevron, du Pont, Exxon, and Texaco give an excessive representation of the oil, gasoline, and chemical sector. Ditto for Alcoa, Boeing, and United Technologies for the aeroplane sector. By contrast there is no media/television/publishing (except coincidentally from General Electric and Disney) representative. Neither is there any company principally supplying food or raw materials, except, coincidentally, for the "junk food" marketed by Philip Morris. And are Sears and Woolworth the best representatives for today's consumer retail marketers? Is AT&T a better representative of the telephone industry than its burgeoning offspring? These anomalies lead many major investment specialists to rely on other market indexes rather than the pyschologically popular Dow.

Here are the twenty stocks included in the Dow Transportation Average:

AMR Corp. (United Airlines)
Airborne Freight Corp.
Alaska Air Group Inc.
America President Cos. Ltd.
Burlington Northern Inc.
CSX Corp.
Carolina Freight Corp.
Consolidated Freightways Inc.
Consolidated Rail Corp. (Conrail)
Delta Airlines Inc.

Federal Express Corp.
Norfolk Southern Corp.
Roadway Services Inc.
Ryder System Inc.
Santa Fe Pacific Corp.
Southwest Airlines Co.
UAL Corp. (United Airlines)
Union Pacific Corp.
USAir Group Inc.
XTRA Corp.

There is no doubt this list thoroughly covers its industry.

Here are the fifteen stocks in the Dow Utilities Average:

American Electric Power Co. Inc.
ARKLA Inc.
Centerior Energy Corp.
Commonwealth Edison Co.
Consolidated Edison Co. of New York
Consolidated Natural Gas Co.
Detroit Edison Co.
Houston Industries Inc.
Niagara Mohawk Power Corp.
Pacific Gas & Electric Co.
Panhandle Eastern Corp.
Peoples Energy Corp.
Philadelphia Electric Co.
Public Service Enterprise Group Inc.
SCEcorp (Southern California Edison Co.)

Each of the Dow Jones averages is a straightforward price formula with its own divisor, and so too is the sixty-five-stock composite average. The individual divisors are also published daily in a *Journal* footnote.

Some investment professionals prefer an index that includes the stock price, the total number of shares issued, and the volume of trading in each stock. Their favorite is the Standard & Poor's 500 Index.

The Standard & Poor's 500-Stock Index

Standard & Poor's Corp. is best known for its continuous publication of financial data on all corporations and as a rating bureau for corporate and municipal bonds. It also compiles and issues the most widely used stock market index, the *S&P 500*.

The S&P 500 consists of 400 NYSE-listed industrial stocks, including all thirty in the DJIA; twenty-five transportation stocks (railroad, airline, trucking, and air-freight companies); forty utility stocks (electric power, natural gas, natural-gas pipeline, and telephone companies); and forty financials (major New York City banks, other regional banks, insurance, savings banks, personal finance, and a few miscellaneous companies).

It is a base-weighted index, meaning that each component stock represents a certain percentage of the index comparable with its respective market value and total number of shares outstanding. For instance, if the total value (number of shares outstanding multiplied by the trading price) of a company's stock represents X percent of the total market value of all stocks listed on the exchange, that stock will represent the same X percent of the index.

First introduced in 1957, the S&P 500 and the newer S&P 400 (smaller-capitalization companies—62 percent trading NYSE, 35 percent NASDAQ, and 3 percent AMEX) are believed to represent 85 percent of the market value of all stocks trading in the United States. The 500 Index in particular is considered a sounder yardstick for institutional investors and mutual funds to compare their investment records than the thirty-stock DJIA.

In fact, the S&P 500 is used for many investment products. Some mutual funds offer portfolios duplicating the stock index; some pension fund managers allot their investments similarly—all on the theory that any losses won't be any greater and any gains will be as great as the stock market as a whole. In recent years institutional investors have been using the S&P 500 as a buy or sell signal for switching from ownership of the actual stocks to the S&P 500 futures in the same stocks (or vice versa) by what is known as *program trading*, the one-step sale (or purchase) of an entire portfolio worth, perhaps, millions of dollars. In mid-June 1991 a *Wall Street Journal* article estimated that "some 75 percent of the $275 billion now held in indexed portfolios is pegged to the S&P 500."

The New York Stock Exchange Composite Index

Sponsored and compiled continuously during the trading day by the NYSE, the Composite Index includes all stocks listed—compared with thirty for the DJIA and 500 for the S&P—and is thus the most comprehensive yardstick for trading of NYSE-listed shares. It was compiled in 1965 and has been published regularly since 1966, when the market value of all issues was pegged at $756.9 billion, compared with the recent figure of $3.8 trillion. Like the S&P 500, the NYSE Composite index is a weighted index, meaning that company stocks with higher market value (total shares outstanding times trading price) are given a proportionally higher rating. The Index also flags separate figures for stocks included in the Composite, broadly grouped as follows: Industrials, Transport, Utilities, and Finance. Though less frequently quoted, the NYSE Composite Index is considered a sounder yardstick for measuring the institutional investor's performance.

The AMEX Market Value Index

The American Stock Exchange also has a trading index. Begun in 1966 as the Price Change Index, it was changed in 1973 to the Market Value Index with a base level of 100; in 1983, as a result of changes in the components, the base level was halved to 50. This index measures the change in the aggregate market value of 1,063 common shares, ADRs, and warrants (many for common stocks listed on the NYSE) issued by 859 companies, with a current market value of approximately $100 billion. The index excludes stock rights, when-issued stock, and Americus Trusts (a hybrid series that splits dividends and capital gains of major corporate stock into separate investments).

The NASDAQ Index

The National Association of Securities Dealers, which supervises the Over-the-Counter market, has its own collection of market-weighted indexes, the most important of which is the NASDAQ National Market System (NMS) Composite

Index, covering its 2,679 actively traded common stocks of U.S. corporations. NASDAQ's second Composite Securities Index covers all 4,000 NASDAQ listings as well as foreign ADRs and foreign securities, mostly of Canadian companies. NASDAQ also has performance indexes, not routinely published, for special categories of industrial, bank, insurance, other finance, transportation, and utility stocks.

The Wilshire 5,000 Equity Index

There are several other indexes less frequently quoted in the financial press, the most important being the Wilshire 5,000 Equity Index, which actually includes around 5,700 common stocks listed on the NYSE, AMEX, and the NASDAQ NMS, or what a spokesman said was "all common stocks for which daily pricing is available."

13

Earnings, Dividends, and Ex-Dividend

The daily and weekly listings of company earnings are of limited use, unless you have the skills of a CPA or merely use these published figures as an alert signal to dig deeper. The figures can be informative—or misleading, without the full financial statements identifying whether the totals include one-time writeoffs or credits, any set-asides to reserves, how much depreciation is included, and any other such accounting sleight-of-hand.

You can see at a glance, however, whether total sales or revenues are higher (or lower) than the figures for the comparable period a year ago. That, at least, tells you whether the company's market share is growing or shrinking. Ditto for the net income figures, though you still won't know without further digging what may have been deducted legally to arrive at that net figure. As a stockholder you will receive the complete quarterly figures by mail, but rarely until weeks after the ones published in the newspapers on the day of release.

By comparison, dividend reports are an easy read and,

naturally, the longest list comprises those companies declaring a *regular* dividend, or the same as was paid in the previous quarter. Hence I tend to ignore that list and scan the shorter ones, beginning with *irregular* (perhaps an extra or a stock) and proceeding to *increased* (the best of news) and *stock* (a split is coming). Finally, I look at the two bad-news listings: *reduced* and *omitted*.

If you don't wish to follow the daily listings, check *Barron's* once a quarter. The regular stock-chart pages for the NYSE, AMEX, NASDAQ/NMS, and all mutual funds include a column for the latest dividend declaration, as well as the record and payment dates.

If you are going to buy or sell any stocks, the record date is the one to watch because this determines who (the buyer or seller) will get the most recently declared dividend. Since stock exchange rules allow five business days (Saturday, Sunday, and any intervening holidays excluded) for every transaction to be settled (called the *settlement date)*, the dividend receiver is the one listed on the corporate records five days before the record date. Hence, a stock bought on any of the four days before the record date is said to be *ex-dividend*, simply meaning the new buyer will *not* get the most recently declared dividend.

This is an even more important consideration when buying or selling mutual funds: Whenever a fund pays a dividend or distributes any capital gains, the net asset value of the shares automatically drops on the same day by the total amount of the distribution. For example, say the fund declares a $1.20 dividend, and five days before the record date the net asset value is $25.00. On the first ex-dividend date the shares would begin trading at $23.80, and the previous owner (usually the fund manager) would pocket the difference. If

Q Is there any relationship between a company's earnings and its price/earnings ratio?

A Fidelity's Peter Lynch in his *One Up on Wall Street* offers a very succinct formula: "A company with an earnings growth rate of 12 percent a year and a p/e ratio of 6 percent a year is a very attractive prospect. On the other hand, a company with a growth rate of 6 percent a year and a p/e ratio of 12 is an unattractive prospect and headed for a comedown."

Q With regard to buying mutual fund shares for a tax-deferred retirement account, need I pay attention to the ex-dividend date?

A Since no tax is levied against this type of account until withdrawal time, it does not matter whether you buy more shares with or without dividends. In the first case, you'll be credited with the gain and be buying fewer shares, and in the latter you'll be buying more shares for the same amount of money.

you bought before the ex-dividend date, you would be adding unnecessarily to your taxable income for a period when, in fact, you did *not* own the shares. So before buying find out a fund's annual declaration dates and buy *after* the shares are ex-dividend. Similarly, if you are selling, do so four days *before* the record date; otherwise you will only get $23.80 a share in our selected example.

Every day *The Wall Street Journal* prints a list of the major listed stocks that will be trading ex-dividend on the following trading day. This list is found beneath the daily "Corporate Dividend News" chart. Mutual funds usually have scheduled dates for dividends and capital-gain distributions and will provide the record dates.

CHART 13

Dividends and Ex-Dividend

Apart from the good (or bad) news about a pending dividend payment, the most important information included in this daily chart is the "record date," or, more simply, who will get the newly declared cash or stock payment.

Traditionally, a buyer and the seller are allowed five trading days to settle the deal. It is only on the fifth day that a corporation's agent knows who is the new owner. Hence any stock changing hands four days before the record date will be trading "without dividend" for the new owner. Only when the next quarterly declaration is made will the new owner benefit. *The Wall Street Journal* publishes daily with its dividend chart a list of those stocks that will be trading "ex-dividend" on the next market day.

The various payment methods as presented here are self-explanatory.

DIVIDEND NEWS

Company	Period	Amt.	Payable date	Record date
		REGULAR		
AmSouth Bancorp	Q	.26	10-1-92	9-11
Beneficial $4.30pf	S	2.15	9-30-92	9-1
Beneficial $5.50pf	Q	1.37½	10-31-92	10-1
Biocraft Labs	A	.10	11-18-92	10-14
Centennial Svgs Bk	Q	.10	9-30-92	9-8
Champion Intl	Q	.05	10-13-92	9-18
Continental Copr	Q	.65	9-15-92	8-31
Cyprus Min $3.75pf	Q	.93¾	10-30-92	10-10
Cyprus Minerals	Q	.20	10-30-92	10-10
Dart Group Corp A	Q	.0333	9-18-92	9-2
Delta Natural Gas	Q	.27	9-15-92	9-1
Delta Woodside	Q	.10	9-7-92	8-31
Dial Corp	Q	.28	10-1-92	9-1
Dial Corp $4.75pf	Q	1.18¾	10-15-92	9-15
Dixie Yarns Inc.	Q	.05	9-10-92	9-3
Doughtie's Foods	Q	.04	10-1-92	9-14
Elco Industries	Q	.13	9-15-92	9-1
Filtertek	Q	.06	11-13-92 1	0-30
Fina Inc clA	Q	.80	9-15-92	9-3
1st Commerce Bcshs	Q	.23	10-15-92	9-30
First Fidelity pfB	Q	.53¾	10-1-92	8-31
First Fidelity pfD	Q	1.88	10-1-92	8-31
First Fidelity dep	Q	.66½	10-1-92	8-31
Harmonica Bancorp	Q	.07½	9-30-92	9-14
IMC Fertilizer Crp	Q	.27	9-30-92	9-16
Jacobsen Stores	Q	.12½	10-9-92	9-18

Johnston Indus	Q	.10	9-23-92	9-4
Kimberly-Clark	Q	.41	10-2-92	9-4
Marion Merrell Dow	Q	.25	10-30-92	9-30
McDonald's Corp	Q	.10	9-18-92	8-31
MidConn Bank	Q	.05	9-30-92	9-15
Morgan Stanley Grp	Q	.24	9-23-92	9-3
Ohio Casualty	Q	.67	9-10-92	9-1
Old Repub Intl	Q	.10	9-21-92	9-11
Peoples Bncrp Wor	Q	.32	10-23-92	10-2
Perkin-Elmer Corp	Q	.17	10-1-92	9-2
Phoenix Re Corp	Q	.05	9-18-92	9-4
Pikeville Natl	Q	.19	10-1-92	9-15
Ruddick Corp	Q	.06	10-1-92	9-18
Ruddick $0.56pref	Q	.14	10-1-92	9-18
Springs Indus clA	Q	.30	9-30-92	9-15
Sterling Bncp Ny	Q	.05	9-30-92	9-15
Toro Co	Q	.12	10-12-92	9-25
US Bancorp Oregon	Q	.19	10-1-92	9-11
Valley Forge Corp	Q	.07½	9-15-92	9-4
Wolverine WrldWide	Q	.04	11-2-92	10-1

IRREGULAR

Carolina 1st Cp pf -	—	.52	10-1-92	9-15
Pacificorp pf'92	—	.49½	11-16-92	10-23
Phoenix Re depshs	—	.50	11-1-92	10-16

FUNDS—REITS—INVESTMENT COS—LPS

BanyanMtginv LP II	—	n.15½	9-25-92	9-15
n-Liquidating distribution.				
Invest Co Amer	Q	h.11	9-8-92	9-4
MSA Realty Corp	Q	.15	9-21-92	9-2
NatlSecsNatlBond	M	h.019	8-31-92	8-24
NatlSecsCalTxExmpt	M	h.069	8-25-92	8-25
NatlSecsFedSecsTr	M	h.0605	8-31-92	8-24
NatlSecsTxExmptBd	M	h.056	8-25-92	8-25
Sun Distrib CL clA	M	.091666	9-30-92	9-1
Sun Distrib LP clB	M	.011027	9-30-92	9-1

EXTRA

Ruddick Corp	—	.15	10-1-92	9-18

STOCK

Gyrodyne Co Amer		2%	9-25-92	8-31
Knape & Vogt Mfg		10%	9-11-92	8-31

INCREASED

	-Amounts-			
	New	Old		
Affil Bkshrs Colo	Q	.23	.21	9-15-92	9-1
Beneficial Corp	Q	.70	.65	9-30-92	9-1
Community Bk Sys	Q	.25	.20	10-9-92	9-15
Knape & Vogt Mfg	Q	.16½	.14	9-11-92	8-31
State Auto Finl	Q	.08	.07	9-30-92	9-8

INITIAL

Florida Prog new	Q	.47333	9-20-92	9-4
Home Depot new	Q	.03	9-16-92	9-2

A–Annual; b–Payable in Canadian funds; h–From Income; k–From capital gains; M–Monthly; Q–Quarterly; S–Semiannual.

Chart reproduced with permission from the Associated Press.

14

Tracking the Markets

Every novice investor needs some basic tools of the trade. Many essential ones cost little; others are quite expensive but are often available in libraries. Over the years my required list has included *The Wall Street Journal*, *Barron's*, the annual *Standard & Poor's Stock Guide*, *Forbes*, and the *Value Line Investment Survey*. You may find other equally valuable publications more to your liking, but here are the reasons for my selection.

The Wall Street Journal exists essentially for the financial reader and thus offers the most extensive menu of business and investment news. Equally important, its stock and financial quotation pages offer more information—including each stock's trading symbol—in wider columns and larger, easier-to-read type than any metropolitan daily can afford to use.

Barron's financial weekly is published every Monday but is actually available at many newsstands the previous Saturday morning. This gives you a chance over the weekend to scan both a wealth of business stories and a complete rundown of the past week's market prices. The weekly tabulations of stock market and mutual fund trading are especially useful because the latest dividend declarations and the record and payment dates are included. This permits you to figure the ex-dividend dates (see previous chapter) if you are contemplating any transactions. Nowhere else is this information so readily available.

Even if you don't get *Barron's* regularly, every mutual fund investor should buy the quarterly issues (mid-February, mid-May, mid-August, and mid-November), which feature the *Barron's/Lipper* mutual funds charts covering the past quarter's performance record and other up-to-date data on all stock and municipal bond funds. Each issue includes performance records on a $10,000 investment for the most recent quarter, the year to date, and five years. Additionally, there are fee schedules, phone numbers, and the name of the portfolio manager. It is worth paying the $2.50 newsstand price (versus the $109 annual subscription rate) to avoid having to wait for next week's uncertain mails.

The *Standard & Poor's Stock Guide* is a handy and essential desktop reference for all listed stocks and mutual funds. In addition to providing trading-price ranges for past periods and columns of financial data, the guide describes a company's basic business, and gives its current S&P rating, the market on which it is traded, and the ticker trading symbol. This monthly publication costs $105 a year, but the average investor need buy only the annual edition, which many metropolitan newspapers, through an arrangement with Standard & Poor's, distribute to their readers in early February for a more affordable $5.00 to $6.00.

Forbes magazine, which is published twice a month, offers a good collection of market commentary as well as often pithy and always brief corporate profiles. Even if you don't subscribe or catch it regularly in your local library, every mutual fund investor should purchase its annual stock and bond fund ratings issue ($4.00), published in early September. In addition to the usual and helpful data on the total return during the past ten years, current yield, sales, and expense charges, *Forbes* has a unique "Up" and "Down" market performance rating. The issue also includes a list of fund distributors with their addresses and toll-free phone numbers and plenty of good reading about the mutual fund industry.

A first-time mutual fund investor can't afford to be without the *Guide to Mutual Funds*, published annually by the Investment Company Institute, a Washington-based trade and lobbying group for the industry. It costs $5.00 (1600 M Street NW, Suite 600, Washington, D.C. 20036) and includes details on more than 3,000 funds with assets of an estimated $1.07 trillion. The funds are listed alphabetically and separately in twenty-two categories of investment objectives, from "Aggressive Growth" to "U.S. Government," and the guide includes some of the best and most comprehensible basic facts about mutual fund investing. The main omissions are any data on fees and annual management expenses, but a trade group obviously has to represent all its members and not emphasize any differences.

For the competitive nitty-gritty, you need to own or have library access to a good mutual fund almanac. One of the best, I've found, is *Donoghue's Mutual Fund Almanac* ($34.95, IBC/Donoghue, Box 8008, Ashland, MA 01721-9104). In addition to a complete directory with addresses and toll-free numbers, this volume includes performance records (plus or minus) for the past ten years; figures showing what a $10,000 investment for either five or ten years is worth today; sales and redemption charges; minimum initial investment; annual expense ratios; total assets in each fund; net asset value per share at the end of the past two calendar years; dividend and capital gains distributions for the past two years; whether each fund permits telephone switches to another fund or money fund sponsored by the same family; whether it offers systematic withdrawal plans, IRA, or Keogh retirement programs; and, finally, whether the fund assesses extra 12(b)1 marketing fees (see chapter 8). IBC/Donoghue also publishes a fortnightly *MONEYLETTER* ($109 a year; same address) covering both mutual funds and investing in general.

There are, of course, scores of other investment newsletters available. Two with a conservative bent that I've relied on are the weekly "United & Babson Investment Report" for stock and bond investors ($215 annually), and the fortnightly "United Mutual Fund Selector" for fund investors ($125 annually). Both are published by Babson-United Investment Advisors (101 Prescott Street, Wellesley, MA 02181) and offer free sample issues on request, as do many other investment newsletter publishers. In selecting a subscription newsletter, avoid those published by brokerage houses or other groups whose main interest is selling or supporting certain investments.

There is no need for novice investors to rush out and buy a slew of directories and newsletters; many are already at hand in your local library, and many librarians welcome suggestions to add timely volumes to their business shelves. Two such are *Value Line Investment Survey* and the *Standard & Poor's Stock Reports*. Both are very expensive but are readily available in libraries, brokerage offices, and many banks that also offer investment services.

Value Line rates and analyzes some 1,700 major company

stocks trading on all exchanges, with at least quarterly revisions and updates that are easily understood by the nontechnical investor. The S&P stock sheets are in separate looseleaf binders for NYSE, AMEX, and OTC companies. These, too, are continuously updated and are invaluable guides to stock-price trends, earnings, and dividends, and forecasts on industry futures.

Two reputable nonprofit organizations have been helping individuals and neighborhood investment clubs for many years. They are the American Association of Individual Investors (625 North Michigan Avenue, Chicago, IL 60611) and the National Association of Investment Clubs (1515 East Eleven Mile Road, Royal Oak, MI 48067).

The AAII bills itself as an "independent corporation formed in 1978 for the purpose of assisting individuals in becoming effective managers of their own assets through programs of education, information, and research." Membership costs $49.00 a year and includes many investment tools. The monthly *AAII Journal* evaluates many stocks, especially those not frequently in the news. Once a year members get an updated "Guide to No-Load Mutual Funds." The group sponsors local chapters in major cities, as well as periodic seminars and home-study materials.

The NAIC is best known for helping to organize local investment clubs and supplying necessary instructional materials. An individual membership costs $32.00 annually, while a club membership costs $30.00, plus $9.00 for each member. Any number can set up a club with the help of the regional officers; alternatively, they will put you in touch with an existing club needing more members. Monthly workshops or seminars are scheduled in many cities. The parent organization publishes a monthly magazine, *Better Investing*, and also operates a Low-Cost Investment Program that permits members to buy a few shares of several major corporations or the one share necessary to start a dividend reinvestment program.

Three books are high on my novice-investor reading list. One is Andrew Tobias's *The Only Other Investment Guide You'll Ever Need* ($5.95 paperback; Simon & Schuster). This is a tax-change update of an earlier volume similarly named and is an honest and sometimes irreverent introduction to the world of investments.

The second is *A Random Walk Down Wall Street* ($14.95; W. W. Norton & Co.), written in the early 1970s and revised since by Burton G. Malkiel, then a Princeton University economist, later dean of the Yale Management School, and now back at Princeton. It is still useful and interesting reading for any investor. The history and theories of investments explained include the controversial proposition that a professional stockbroker can do no better consistently than someone picking stocks by throwing darts at the market quotation pages from your newspaper! For the past several years *The Wall Street Journal* has been running an academic contest based on this theory. In 1992 the *Journal* reported that the dart throwers won with their most recent six-month selections and in total have won thirteen times, versus fifteen times for the pros.

For a more contemporary look at the investment scene, read *One Up on Wall Street* ($10.95; Penguin Books) by Peter Lynch, the successful fourteen-year portfolio manager of Fidelity's Magellan Fund. Until Lynch resigned and retired from fund managing in mid-1990, the then $12 billion-plus growth stock fund held the record for the best ten-year performance of any funds. (You can read more about Lynch's book in chapter 20.)

Studying alone isn't the only way to hone your investment skills. Many universities and communities offer adult education courses for very affordable fees. You can usually find a variety of investment topics taught by brokers moonlighting after working hours. This is a good way not only to learn the fundamentals but also to keep up-to-date on investing trends. Be careful, however, to preserve the teacher-student relationship; don't be tempted to become a client.

You will frequently see advertisements for sundry free public seminars sponsored by brokerage houses. The ads invariably say *all welcome...limited seating...phone for reservations.* Don't let this deter you. All they want to know is how large a hotel room to rent, how much cheese and wine to have on hand, and, most importantly, how many supersalesmen to have on duty to back up the featured speaker. Go listen, learn, and ask questions. Take any offered literature and prospectuses and add to your investment study library. But again, as with the adult education teacher, don't become an instant client or sign up for anything at the seminar. Only after studying the material and comparing it with similar products available from other brokers should you decide whether that particular investment fits your goals and diversification plan.

15

Managing Your Investments

The question first-time investors most often ask is: "Do I need a full-service broker?" There are times and reasons to answer "yes," but until we can explore these in detail, the quick answer is "no." For an uncomplicated purchase order of a specific investment, use a discount broker. A discount broker does not offer any advice or manage customer portfolios. No hand-holding means lower costs and transaction fees.

After you decide what stocks and bonds you want to own, scour the Yellow Pages for a list of the nearest discount brokers. Telephone or visit the office of each and ask for their commission on a purchase of X number of shares of the stock you wish to buy. Place your order with the one offering the lowest commission; it's a simple execution and there is very little difference in commission charges between discounters, but their fees are anywhere from two-thirds to one-half less than those of a full-service broker.

When selecting a discounter be certain the office logo, of-

ficial literature, and/or statements include these initial desig-
nations: member of NYSE (the New York Stock Exchange),
NASD (the National Association of Securities Dealers, the
industry's regulator and policeman), and SIPC (the Securities
Investor Protection Corp., the stockbroker's portfolio insurer
and investor's guarantor).

When buying common stock it is less expensive and more
convenient to deal in a round lot, or one hundred shares. The
broker can execute the order immediately without having to
find someone willing to process an "odd lot" (fewer than one
hundred shares), the exchange-floor specialist in this stock
can execute the order immediately at a known market price,
and the same is true later should you want to sell the shares.

If you are a first-time client, you may be asked to deposit
the cost of the shares and commission up front. After you
have established an account there, you normally have five
days until the standard settlement date to pay. If you don't
pay on time, the broker may be obliged to sell the shares and
then bill you for the commissions.

Always insist on having the share certificates delivered or
mailed to you. Ownership certificates are still issued for common and preferred shares and a few bonds, though several recent industry and regulatory studies suggest the day is not far
off when certificates will no longer be issued.

Most Treasury, corporate, and municipal bonds and all mutual funds are now registered only in the records of the issuer
or the issuer's agent-trustee. Your periodic statements are the
only record of investments owned. It is therefore essential to
receive and keep on file all transaction statements, normally
dated and mailed the same day as any stocks and bonds are
bought or sold. If you have not received them within five business days (Saturday and Sunday excluded), immediately check

Q Are there different categories of stock purchase orders?

A Yes. The most routine one is a *market order*, an order to buy or to sell at the most advantageous price immediately available. Then there is the *limit order*, an order to buy or sell at a specified price or a better price then the current one, if obtainable. Finally, there is the *stop order*, an order to buy at a price above or sell at a specified price below the current market. Covering all three categories is a *GTC order* (good 'til canceled), indicating that any one of the previous orders remains in effect until either executed or canceled.

Q How can I build a stock portfolio with dividends spread out instead of arriving all at once?

A Twice during the year the *United & Babson Investment Report* (101 Prescott Street, Wellesley, MA 02181) has a feature listing high-quality stocks with established payouts providing a stream of dividends every week or fortnight. If you don't like their selections, study the Standard & Poor's *Stock Guide* (often available through your local newspaper in late January) or *Barron's* financial weekly and pick six stocks with payment dates approximately on the first and fifteenth of January, February, and March; the payment cycle repeats itself each quarter thereafter. If you prefer a weekly check, follow the same process and select thirteen stocks.

back with the broker. Routinely and thoroughly compare the transaction statements against your monthly account reports.

If you are building your portfolio with mutual funds, it is not necessary to buy lots of one hundred shares. Rather, decide on the management company and the diversification desired. As mentioned in chapter 8, aggressive and small capitalization funds are most appropriate for the younger investor, a mix of capital appreciation and income is recommended for those with families, and a preponderance of income funds and a few stock funds with capital-appreciation potential would be a sound mix for older investors.

In each category buy as many shares as available investment money permits and then sign up for the fund's dividend reinvestment plan for the automatic acquisition of more shares from capital gains and dividend distributions. Or if you foresee a periodic need for this income, open an interest-paying money market account with the same management, and these distributions will automatically be credited to you and will be readily available to withdraw by check or to invest in other funds.

In selecting individual mutual funds, my own preference is for no-loads, those that do not have a purchase charge (e.g., T. Rowe Price, Scudder, and Vanguard among major fund managers). Equally well known are funds managed by Fidelity and Dreyfus, which each has low loads, varying by fund from 2 to 4 percent.

If you are buying individual stocks, it is also recommended that you immediately sign up for the company's dividend reinvestment plan. This is an inexpensive way to acquire additional shares without any brokerage charges. If the sum of your quarterly dividend payment is not enough to buy a full share or an even number of shares, the company's book entry statement will show ownership of a fractional share.

Many brokerage houses also offer a variety of variously titled portfolio-building plans, often involving a contractual agreement to add a certain dollar amount to the account each month. Certain mutual fund sponsors have similar investment packages. In fact, we have entered an era in which lines of distinction between banking and investing are fast disappearing, so it pays for some investors to have a full-service broker.

Full-service brokerage accounts offer the following advantages:

- They permit you to buy and sell any investments with a single telephone call. Ownership of the stocks, bonds, or securities is registered in the firm's street name to your account. (This eliminates the need to hold certificates in a safe deposit box and deliver them to the broker when a sale is planned.) Since brokers hold stocks and bonds for many clients, they routinely monitor for any early call dates of bonds or deadlines for tendering stocks being acquired.
- They facilitate buying stocks on margin or short-selling, since about half of the trading value of your in-house portfolio is accessible collateral. (But be aware of possible *margin calls* to put up more money or stock of a certain value immediately should a sharp drop in the stock market reduce the value of your street-name collateral below a standard 50 percent of any commitments.)
- They can include a *cash sweep* component, similar to an interest-earning money market fund, into which all dividends and interest payments are deposited on the actual payment dates, not some days later, when the mail arrives and payment checks have to be deposited in some other banking account.
- They often have check-writing or credit-card charge privileges with interest charges on any outstanding balances at the lower *broker's loan rate* (usually the same as the prime lending rate at national banks).

These multipurpose accounts are available from full-service brokers and some nationwide discount brokers, such as Fidelity Investments, Quick & Reilly Group, and Charles Schwab & Co. The only difference between the two types of brokers is the extent to which the broker helps you decide on your investments. The discounter efficiently executes your orders; the full-service broker recommends and supervises.

If you want a broker, select carefully and wisely. When you sign up with a brokerage house, the office manager will assign a broker to your account. This will invariably be the newest or youngest member of the staff, who has the shortest client list. Now is the time for you to establish the ground rules for your relationship. At the first interview decide if the chemistry is right—whether you feel you will be comfortable doing business with this person. If not, ask the manager to assign someone else to your account.

Inquire about the broker's credentials and experience. If you want to check these answers, a telephone call to the local office of the National Association of Securities Dealers and/or the Securities division of your state government will disclose whether the broker is a registered representative and whether he or she has been involved in any disciplinary action. (For the addresses and telephone numbers of each, see Appendix D.)

Plainly state what your investment goals are and what risks you are prepared to take.

Insist that the broker thoroughly explain the ups and downs, the risks and rewards, of any investment being considered. If you don't understand, don't invest. If the promised returns sound too good to be true, they are; don't bite. (For instance, in recent years single-premium, tax-deferred annuities and limited partnerships were two investment products pushed by all major brokerage houses as being high-return investments. Many of both have collapsed, and gullible clients have lost millions of dollars. Most brokers and financial planners knew little about these products except that they earned them very high commissions.)

When considering an investment, frankly ask who gets what part of the commission. Remember, it's your money; don't be afraid to ask questions, and never permit yourself to be intimidated.

Most importantly, *never* give a broker discretionary power over your account. You need to know what is being bought and sold, when and why. Otherwise the broker is free to trade at will or do what is known as *churning* an account to generate commissions—and, not infrequently, losses.

It is not unlikely that at some time you will think your account has been mishandled. In many, or even most, cases these minor or major disputes can be settled within the branch office or the headquarters of the brokerage company.

First, request an appointment with the compliance officer. Each brokerage has one such person who is instructed to hear all client complaints and, if possible, mediate. If this fails, take your problem to the officer manager. If you have been twice thwarted, request the name of the compliance officer at the company's headquarters. When contacting this person, be sure to supply sufficient documentation to support your complaint. If the headquarters compliance officer offers you a dollar sum representing only a portion of your loss, do not be in a hurry to accept.

(I remember one case in which a major national brokerage house offered an unhappy client $5,000 to compensate for a $20,000 loss from too-risky investments. Eventually, with some third-party nudging, the case was settled with full repayment, plus interest. This brokerage house knew it was in the wrong or it would not have made the first offer to repay $5,000, but hoped to settle the dispute at the lowest cost.)

If you should encounter similar reluctance to settle and

still feel your claim is just, turn next to the compliance offices of the stock exchanges. Every broker is a member of the New York and American stock exchanges and accepts responsibility to arbitrate any disagreements. Similarly, consider getting help from the National Association of Securities Dealers, the industry's policeman and supervisor of the Over-the-Counter markets. (See addresses in Appendix B.)

Whether you have a regular broker or periodically use a discounter, there is one cardinal rule for any investor: Never buy anything as the result of a phone solicitation. If you know the broker, request that a prospectus be sent to you and tell the broker that you'll think it over. If you don't know the broker, he or she is doing what the trade labels a *cold call* (i.e., keep dialing until you find a sucker!). Hang up.

Remember, all brokers need to make a week's wage. They are in business to generate commissions and, secondarily, to service your account. Their employers inevitably have blocks of newly issued investments that they must unload. Only later in your investing career, when you are sufficiently knowledgeable and ready to try more risky but more profitable vehicles, will you need to find a reputable specialist broker and grant her or him free rein to invest your money.

16

Keeping Records

O ne of the most routine and least difficult investment chores is keeping records; conversely—and not surprisingly—failure to do so ultimately causes the novice the most trouble, money, and tax credits.

The first and most important document to file is the original stock or fund purchase confirmation order. This gives both the price per share and the total commission charge for the transaction.

Both figures are necessary to determine your original per-share cost basis. For example, let's say you bought 200 shares of XYZ company for $17.00 each. In reality the shares cost $17.50 after adding on the $100 broker's fee. You later sell these shares for $25.00 per share, with the same $100 broker's fee, for an actual capital gain of $1,400, *not* the $1,600 fixed in your mind.

This may sound like penny-pinching but could represent substantial savings when claiming capital gains (or losses). The Internal Revenue Service is not the ogre we tend to label it. It does, though, expect some reasonable documentation or acceptable evidence of ballpark estimates.

There is one such method for those selling shares of common stocks who have kept no records, or others who have shares inherited long ago from Uncle Harry. Settle on the year, check the *Wall Street Journal* stock-page microfilms, and get a trading price for the first and last days of that year. Then use an average of the two figures as the per-share cost basis for figuring a capital gain or loss. Don't forget to factor in your transaction fees.

Normally, you should be able to get an accurate cost basis for inherited shares, such as Uncle Harry's, from the estate executor, because all such stocks have a stepped-up market value as of the date of death, and this price would be included in the executor's inventory. If, however, any investments were received as a gift during the donor's lifetime, the donor's original cost basis is your cost basis no matter when the stock is sold. That's why it is important to keep purchase statements or ask Uncle Harry for the correct figure.

If any holdings are sold or withdrawn from a tax-deferred pension account (i.e., the sums were not subject to tax at the time of contribution) such as an Individual Retirement Account, 401k (employer-employee benefit plan), or 403b (for teachers and other municipal employees) plan, there is no need except personal interest for meticulous record keeping. You are taxed on the specific sums withdrawn, without consideration for the cost.

If, though, you are making withdrawals from an IRA or a single-premium annuity account to which you have made contributions with income already taxed, it is essential to keep these contribution records. In these cases only the compounded interest earned or capital gain realized are subject to tax.

Q I am going to inherit about $100,000 in stocks, bonds, and a small amount of cash from my mother's estate. What is the tax liability if I liquidate everything and use the proceeds to buy a home?

A Normally there is no tax liability to the recipient for inherited stocks, bonds, and cash. The estate executor would pay anything due based on his or her original acquisition cost. If the stocks and bonds were sold when transferred, the only possible gain (or loss) would be the difference between the estate's valuation and the then–market trading prices.

Q What is the age limit for someone to be considered a minor? Can we give our son, a twenty-year-old college student, his tuition under the "gifts to minors acts"? How can we show this on our income tax return?

A Age eighteen is the benchmark for national voting privileges under the Twenty-sixth Amendment to the Constitution, adopted in 1971. The age specified in the numerous "gifts to minors acts" of the states varies from eighteen to twenty-one. This does not create any income tax deduction but does mean that your control over any gifts (money, stocks, or bonds) is relinquished at that age. Although you get no tax credit, you cannot give your son (or anyone) more than $10,000 a year (or $20,000 from both parents) without incurring a liability for a gift tax, subject to a $600,000 lifetime maximum.

Record keeping gets more complicated when you have been participating in dividend reinvestment plans for corporate common stocks or shares in mutual funds. You know how much you originally invested, as well as the broker's commission or a fund's front-end load charge, so keep records of dividends and capital gains declared each year and divide that sum by the number of new shares acquired. Keep a running tally of each year's additions. A filer of an IRS Form 1040 would normally do this annually to identify taxable income other than wages. Short-form filers may only identify the total sum of "other income" and so should therefore keep their own records until such time as the investment is sold and a capital gain (or loss) is declared. There are other acceptable methods for figuring the cost basis of mutual fund shares acquired at different times and prices. These computations are best left to your tax accountant or lawyer. If you have accurate records of what shares were acquired and at what price, you can designate specific shares to be sold out of the total holdings.

Mutual fund investors may get some help in the future with cost-basis calculations. A U.S. House of Representatives tax committee is considering a bill requiring mutual funds to provide cost-basis figures when shares are sold. A universal methodology would be a great help, but the canny investor should still learn how to cross-check the fund's figures.

This same alertness is recommended for any bank, brokerage, or fund statements. Check them as soon as they are received. Errors do occur, even in this computer-driven age, and if you don't have them corrected immediately, it takes forever to do so.

You also need the cost-basis figures when claiming tax credits for permissible investment gifts to charitable organizations. Even though you are allowed to deduct the full market value on the date of the transfer, the listing of the acquisition cost is just another way for IRS auditors to check that you were the legal owner.

Stock splits present another challenge for the record keeper. At the time new certificates are received or show up on your brokerage statements, pencil in the adjusted cost basis for all the shares now held. (If you have failed to do this, a handy reference is the *Capital Changes Reports*, published and regularly updated by the Commerce Clearing House Inc. This volume would be available only in a brokerage house or business school library.)

Similarly, acquisitions by tender offers, such as the Chemical Bank takeover of Manufacturer's Hanover, or divestitures, such as the 1984 AT&T split-up and creation of seven independent regional Bells, require immediate recording of the new stock cost. Save the announcement statements from the principal corporation and, preferably, mark an adjusted price on any certificates—old ones diluted or new ones issued. Stockholder service departments are rarely interested in helping you reconstruct the value of stocks many splits ago.

If you are required to tender shares in a takeover, there are a couple of safeguards to follow: make photocopies of both the certificate(s) and the signed tender form; and send the package by registered, insured mail with a "return receipt requested." (This is a postcard signed by an authorized person at the tender office and is your guarantee that the mail was delivered. It will cost you a few dollars, but consider the sum well spent.)

If, perchance, you can't find the stock certificate, contact the stockholder service office of the issuing corporation, or sometimes a stock solicitation company retained by the corporation. If your name is listed on a current stockholder list and you have been receiving dividends or financial statements, you will have little trouble arranging a replacement. You will be required to file certain papers and pay a bonding premium covering the value of the stock to protect the company should the original certificate prove to have been stolen, forged, and sold.

17

A Widow's Dilemma

In the "old days" few wives were kept up-to-date about family finances. A husband's all-too-familiar "I'll take care of it" may have been a convenient routine, but tragically has left too many women unprepared for widowhood. The catch-up learning about and sorting out of family investments may seem an overwhelming task. It shouldn't and won't be, however, if it is undertaken calmly and methodically.

The first chore is to compile an inventory of all investments, including any old stock certificates, held in one's spouse's name or jointly. It's more than likely that an executor will help with this task in the course of preparing an estate tax return.

If you know little or nothing about the various holdings, don't be in a rush to sell. It is better to have them all reregistered in your own name and to wait until you can evaluate the portfolio and your own need for income.

Reregistering the certificates is a simple procedure. Send the stock or bond certificate and a copy of the death certificate to the secretary of the corporation or its agent and have the signature on your cover letter of instructions certified (or what is called guaranteed) by your commercial bank or a stockbroker. (Because of outdated stock exchange rules, signature verification by a savings bank is not acceptable.) Be certain that you keep photocopies of all these documents and send them by registered, insured mail, return receipt requested. If there is a will or trust with specific instructions, a lawyer or trustee will presumably help.

If any lump-sum payments are received from insurance companies or pension sponsors, put the cash promptly into a bank certificate of deposit or U.S. Treasury securities with maturities selected for times when your affairs are sorted out. The longer the term, the higher the interest earnings. Similarly, do not leave any uncashed checks lying about. Deposit them on the day they are received into your own bank account. There is no reason why the issuer should receive daily interest on these checks when you could benefit, however small the sum.

After things have calmed down, it is portfolio appraisal time. In addition to any certificates found in a safe deposit box, hunt for any statements for brokerage or mutual fund accounts. You probably will find a mixture of old bonds (maybe some with coupons attached that must be clipped and submitted through a bank on interest-payment dates), recognizable corporate stocks and mutual funds, and some lesser-known stocks that may either be comers or ones long dead.

If the estate executor has not given you a statement of the current market value of all these holdings, try to determine what each is worth today by checking the quotation pages in the newspaper or asking brokers. (Nowadays fewer bonds are listed on exchanges and even fewer trading prices are reported regularly, so you will need to contact a broker.)

Q At my husband's death I was the sole beneficiary of our joint holdings, including 1,000 shares of stock. All of these shares were subsequently reregistered in my name. I now am selling 400 shares. Is my cost basis computed as of the estate-tax filing date or the original date of purchase?

A A combination of both. Let's say these 1,000 shares cost $10 each, or $10,000 total, and had a death-date value of $20 per share. Your half of the joint holding, or 500 shares, would have the same $10 original cost basis. Your late husband's 500 shares (now in your name only) would have a date-of-death cost basis of $20. If you have a separate certificate for the new inherited shares, you could sell 400 of those and claim a $20 cost per share. If not, there would be a combined cost basis of $15 (500 shares at $10 and 500 inherited shares at $20).

Q Years ago my late husband gave me 100 shares of a mutual fund. Now I have about 350 shares and would like to give them to my three grandchildren to help them with future college expenses. I don't want to sell the shares and pay taxes. How should I handle this?

A The sponsor of the mutual fund will gladly assist you in setting up three separate accounts in each grandchild's name under the state's Uniform Gifts to Minors Act. If you wish you can be named as custodian, or (preferably) you can designate a parent as custodian. You will not incur any tax liability, but the shares and any interest earnings will be irrevocably out of your control.

Q I am an eighty-nine-year-old woman and have 1,000 shares of a high-quality, dividend-producing stock. For additional income, should I sell?

A Sell one hundred shares at a time, both to minimize any capital gain and to produce the needed income.

Some older bonds paying low interest rates by current standards may be close enough to maturity that they will be redeemed at full face value and will thus be worth holding a while longer. Others will have to be considered separately on the basis of date-of-death market value, interest rate, and maturity or first early call date.

Common stocks are easier to sort out. Companies with recognizable names and a history of dividend and stock-price gains are worth holding, regardless of the current stock market gyrations and ever-changing ratings by analysts. Lesser-known stocks with marginal market value, little history, and even less regular reporting can be put away for later research or forgotten.

Any mutual fund holdings are even easier to decide about. The net asset values are reported daily, and there are enough sources for comparative performance records (*The Wall Street Journal, Barron's/Lipper, Forbes*, etc.—see chapter 14) to help you decide whether to sell or hold.

Whatever you decide after completing a portfolio appraisal, don't make the mistake of holding on to all these sundry stocks and bonds, Treasuries, and mutual funds just because your spouse picked them. Some may have been hot tips that are best forgotten, some may have been start-ups that once showed more promise than now, and some may have been established stocks with a predictable chance for stock-price gains. Sell stocks with substantial capital gains, since the date-of-death market price establishes a much lower cost basis than the purchase price and more than likely will wipe out any tax liability.

Next, redirect all investments to your new income needs and long-term goals. Now is also the time to decide whether you want to handle your own investments or have someone else do it. Whatever your choice, don't give the job to a relative; too often this results in more than just portfolio losses.

Many widows turn to bank trust departments. This is certainly safe, convenient, and orderly. But unless the portfolio or investable cash is substantial, you won't get any special attention. All trust funds are lumped and invested much as in a mutual fund, with about the same returns and risks, depending on the investments selected. But unlike a mutual fund, a bank's portfolio bundling service will probably cost you the standard (and I think unconscionable) 6 percent of assets annually. This means that the value of the portfolio has to increase 6 percent each year before you get a cent. If you already have an arrangement with a bank trust department and want to leave it that way, try to renegotiate the annual fee as a percent of earnings, not assets.

Other widows turn their portfolios and other assets over to stockbrokers or financial planners. Either course entails an unnecessary expense and is sometimes even a prescription for financial disaster. The first loyalty of such professionals is naturally to themselves and the commissions they can generate. Similarly, never do business with an unknown broker, no matter how fancy-sounding the company name.

I think the best choice is to put your assets into a mutual fund, preferably a no-load fund (see chapter 8). You will have some of the country's best professionals tending your assets for the modest annual management fees of one-half to 1 percent. Determine your risk tolerance and then select a diversified portfolio to meet your income needs.

As mentioned in chapter 8, older persons should concentrate on investing for income. Select bond and utility stock funds with a smaller portion of the total in so-called balanced funds—a mix of stocks and bonds to offset each other's periodic ups or downs in response to changing interest rates.

Since the longevity odds favor women in our society, it is important for every widow or wife to be familiar with the family's assets and debts. If your spouse has not compiled such a list for you, insist he do so now. This day. The list should include:

- a rundown of all debts—mortgages, bank loans, auto loans, credit-card balances, and due dates for payments;
- a rundown of recurring payments for property taxes and federal and state quarterly estimated income taxes;
- data on any private or public pensions and the addresses of the administrators;
- insurance policies in force and where the policies are located;
- location of the will, if one exists;
- location of any stock or bond certificates and other investment data; and
- information on any brokerage accounts, including whether the broker has discretionary authority to trade. (If so, cancel that authority, at least until some later date.)

Old stock certificates were mentioned at the beginning of this chapter. You may be wondering what to do with any found in your spouse's desk or your bank box, since it is fairly certain that none will be included on an executor's appraisal list, nor are you likely to find a quotation in the newspaper financial pages. But before you relegate any to a wallpapering project, it may be profitable to do a little research.

Sometimes companies change names, or they are acquired and the stock is exchanged or paid off. Occasionally stockholders who have changed addresses fail to receive notice of this and are listed as *address unknown* on the stockholder's list turned over to transfer agents. Dividends, if any, just accumulate as undeliverable. Old railroad bonds in particular have been tangled in acquisitions or years-long legal battles; eventually a payoff price is established and the money is held in an independent escrow account until claimed.

How do you find out if an old certificate has any value? There is an easy but expensive way: Pay a stock and bond tracer. Or a time-consuming but fun way: Play detective.

The sleuthing begins with a quick check of the weekly stock market quotations, particularly the Over-the-Counter pages in your Sunday newspaper or *Barron's*. If you find nothing there, locate a business school library that has the semiannual volumes of the *National Stock Summary*. These are compiled and published by the National Quotation Bureau and distributed daily as the pink sheets to subscribing brokers. The *National Stock Summary* gives data on name changes, mergers, last bid and ask prices, and the like, creating a trail to follow. If your stock is not included in the most recent issue, check back issues for five, ten, or more years, as names of inactive stocks are eventually deleted.

Another excellent source, especially for old mining and railroad companies, is the sixteen-volume set of *Scudder-Fisher Manuals*, first published in 1927 and still being compiled by one of the founder's sons, Robert D. Fisher, now a vice-president of R. M. Smythe & Co., the nation's oldest—and still leading—stock tracer.

A final and often promising trail begins at the securities office of the state in which your old company was incorporated. (This information is printed on the certificate.) Some states will accept phone inquiries; others will respond only to a written request and charge a modest fee. Delaware, the current preferred state for incorporation, has installed a "voice box" telephone system in its securities information division that shunts you through a maze of recorded "punch number X" instructions without ever reaching a person. This chain of recorded messages too often just produces a morning of frustration without any answers. Consequently, regardless of the state of incorporation, I suggest you write, enclosing a photocopy (never send an original) of the certificate and a stamped, self-addressed return envelope with your information request. (See Appendix C for addresses of state securities offices.)

Some stock research specialists suggest that state securities offices should be the first research stop, simply because if any money is being held in escrow for currently inactive stocks or bonds after varying numbers of years, it will have been turned over to the states under escheat or abandoned property laws. If no owner or claimant is found, the moneys eventually are turned over to the state.

There is no guarantee that any of these searches will pay off. If they do not, and you still want a conclusive answer, send a photocopy of the certificate and a $50 check to R. M. Smythe & Co. (26 Broadway, New York, NY 10004). Within a reasonable time, Smythe will send you a written report of the stock's value and last-known status of the old company as well as an appraisal of the certificate's possible value as a collectible. Those certificates with signatures of old industrial barons are especially valuable. Smythe also sponsors international auctions and trade fairs for collectors of coins, stamps, and financial memorabilia.

18

Retirement Savings

There was a time when a wage earner assumed that a company pension plus Social Security benefits would be enough for a comfortable retirement income. Thanks to years of inflation and a shorter period of superinflation, this is no longer the case. Nowdays, anyone hoping to enjoy both the basic necessities and occasional luxuries, as well as to keep pace with a minimal inflation rate, should build and nurture a nest egg for postretirement years.

How these sums are invested is more a question of preference and is less important than the habit of saving. A few years ago the tax-deductible Individual Retirement Accounts (IRAs) were the thrifty person's dream. Unfortunately, Congress shot down that dream in 1986 with another tax-code change. But if the then-permissible $2,000 a year had been invested annually and been allowed to grow at a modest 6 percent for thirty years, it would have represented about $200,000. If the same sum had been invested in common stocks, which historically have represented total returns (dividends and capital gains reinvested) of 10 percent, the IRA sum would have totaled more than $400,000.

This suggests that if you still have an IRA with several years until permissible withdrawals (not before age 59½) in a bank CD, now would be the time to switch this sum into a mutual fund IRA or a self-directed brokerage IRA to buy stocks. You can do so without penalty any time within sixty days of canceling a maturing CD.

IRAs are still legal without the tax credit—and there is even talk in Congress about reviving them as an annual deduction. Whatever the outcome of this revival effort, anyone who can afford to save an extra $2,000 a year should keep an IRA going, first because all earnings and capital gains are not taxed until withdrawn; and second, because if you should need the principal for any reason, that sum can be withdrawn without penalty while the accrued interest remains tax-deferred.

Funds from either type of IRA can be withdrawn without penalty any time after age 59½. You can withdraw the entire amount saved or any portion of it, but income tax at your bracket rate will be due on any amount taken out. Unless you need the funds, I'd advise leaving the accounts intact until mandatory withdrawals, beginning with the year in which you reach age 70½. That is to say, if your seventieth birthday occurs in the first six months of a year, you will have to start withdrawals before year end. If it occurs in the second half of the year, withdrawals can be postponed until the appropriate six-month date of the following year. Irrespective of the precise legal withdrawal date, I'd suggest that you start in your seventieth birthday year because all subsequent withdrawals must be made by December 31 of the tax year, and it is possible that you will have to make two withdrawals—and incur two tax liabilities—in the same year.

Q   Is it possible for an individual taxpayer to establish and maintain an Individual Retirement Account through the purchase of U.S. securities directly from the Federal Reserve Bank?

A   No. Each IRA must have a trustee to do the paperwork and keep tabs on your eventual tax liability for the IRS. You can, though, have an IRA invested only in U.S. securities through a mutual fund or a self-directed brokerage account.

Q   I am seventy-five years old, and my wife and I have slightly more than $400,000 in liquid assets (money market funds, U.S. Treasuries, and good common stocks). I also have an insurance policy worth $27,000 (originally $52,000 before I took some 5 percent loans) on which I'm paying an $1,800 annual premium. Is there any point in keeping this policy in force? I say no; my wife says yes.

A   A quick check of the longevity charts indicates you've already had your three score and ten years, and with all these liquid assets, I'd drop the discussion and book two first-class tickets on a luxury liner heading around the world.

The sums withdrawn are based on your own life expectancy and the assumption that the government can recover the deferred tax liability before you die. Since this date is more uncertain than taxes, you are allowed to combine your life expectancy with that of a spouse (or any other beneficiary) so that the mandatory annual withdrawal sums are lower, and the value of the IRA can continue compounding. You can always withdraw more than the required annual minimum and pay the tax due, but once the minimum sum is set, your spouse or beneficiary is stuck with that schedule.

Since the demise of tax-deductible IRAs, more and more companies have created 401(k) retirement savings plans. The growing popularity of 401(k)s is probably a forewarning that pension plans of the future may not be as liberal as in the past, and employees should start paying more attention to individual saving plans.

These come in numerous varieties, but the essential features are a reduction in taxable income each year, and tax deferral until retirement on both the principal and any earnings or capital appreciation of your own contributions and any from your employer.

Some company 401(k)s are structured simply around employee-only contributions; others have matching features, with company cash contributions added on an all-employee wage formula; others offer a dollar value of the company stock to match cash deductions from your wages; still others have a profit-sharing centerpiece. The structures are endless, but regardless of the specific formula, sign up; otherwise you will pay the same sum in added taxes.

Most 401(k)s offer investment choices, frequently restricted to a guaranteed investment contract (GIC), which in effect is the same as an insurance annuity with a fixed interest rate for one year, which is reset annually, and a stock mutual fund. If you have a choice, select the stock fund with the chance for capital appreciation and inflation matching.

Most state and municipal workers and educational employees of these public entities are offered participation in 403(b) retirement saving programs. These predate 401(k)s and operate similarly. Unfortunately, most offer few investment choices. If you have the option, select stock-fund investments, again to match inflation and gain capital.

Investing is only half the game. What do you do when you stop working? Most plans give you several choices:

- Leave your account assets in the plan as a retiree. No new contributions will be made, but if you are satisfied with past earnings and the plan's managers, stay put.

- Take a lump-sum payment equal to the value of any and all contributions in your name. If you select, or are forced to select, this option, make certain that the entire sum is used to open a new IRA within sixty days. Otherwise it will all be added to your taxable income for that year.

- Split the assets, particularly if you have been acquiring company stocks either on a matching basis, through profit sharing, or through an employees stock ownership plan (ESOP). If you have confidence that the company is well run and has a good future, take any cash assets for a new IRA and leave the stocks credited to your name under the company 401(k) umbrella. If you doubt the company's future, either have them convert your equity into cash, or take delivery of stock certificates and cash assets and transfer both into a self-directed brokerage IRA.

- Convert your plan assets into an annuity with a schedule of monthly payments. This alternative, which is offered—even encouraged—by many 403(b) plans, is acceptable if the insurance company issuing the annuity has a credible financial history. If it is a company with questionable financial stability, try to arrange transfer of assets to a well-established and unquestionably solvent company.

United States Series E Savings Bonds were the granddaddy of retirement savings for many families since they were first launched in 1941. They didn't pay much interest but were easy to accumulate through payroll deductions or at the neighborhood bank.

When the interest-rate formula was changed in 1982 and

the new Series EE were issued, the bonds became a very competitive investment for the smaller-sum and regular saver. Those holding either Series E on extended maturity or the new Series EE for no fewer than five years have been earning an average of 8.18 percent for the past ten years. These variable interest rates are set effective each May 1 and November 1 and are equal to 85 percent of the interest rate on U.S. Treasury securities with five years to maturity. The two six-month rates set in 1991 were 6.57 percent for bonds issued April 1 to October 31 and 6.38 percent for bonds issued from November 1 to April 30, 1992, effectively earning more than other savings accounts if held for five years. Under present regulations a minimum of 6 percent will be paid on all bonds no matter the variable floor rates.

In 1989 the U.S. Treasury tidied up another uncertainty about final maturity dates, or when outstanding bonds would no longer be earning interest. Under these new regulations, any Series E bonds issued before December 1965 have a maximum life of forty years from the date of issue. Those Series E and EE bonds issued after November 1965 stop earning interest exactly thirty years from date of issue.

In either case these maturing bonds can be converted to the new Series HH bonds within one year from final maturity date in increments of no less than $500. When this is done, the Series E or EE holder has the option of either paying the federal tax on the accrued interest or postponing this tax liability day until the HH bonds are cashed or mature. Thereafter, though, the 6 percent current interest is paid semiannually on the Series HH bonds and must be included in the taxable income for that year.

All Series H bonds issued between 1959 and 1979 reach final maturity exactly thirty years from the date of issue, and

Series HH issued in 1980 and thereafter have a maximum life of exactly twenty years from the date of issue.

There is no limit on the total maximum investment in U.S. bonds, but the annual purchase limit is $30,000 per individual. It's a good bet for Uncle Sam, who has borrowed some $125 billion at comparatively low interest rates, and a better bet for those who wish to postpone any federal tax liability and to avoid completely any state or local income tax.

19

Investments to Avoid

There are many, many more investments for the technically knowledgeable or risk-inclined investor. Fortunes are made—and lost—daily, but for the novice most are crapshoots with about the same results. Except in very general terms, I am not qualified to write about them and you are not qualified to invest until you become more savvy. Suffice it to mention the traditional ones, mostly to identify the risks.

The oldest and one of the fastest games in Chicago and a few other cities is commodity futures trading. Essentially there are two types of players: the hedgers and the speculators.

The hedgers are the nation's farmers, who want to be sure at planting time that they can sell their grains for a reasonable price at harvest time. Or the cereal makers, who will be buying the grain on an orderly schedule. Or the silversmiths, who will need the metal for manufacturing their products during the year. Or any number of other providers of grains, metals, and other consumer products such as coffee, cocoa, gasoline, and heating oil.

On the other side of the transactions are the speculators, who never intend to take delivery of a carload of anything. In between is the clearinghouse, known as the buyer to all sellers and the seller to all buyers, simply because at the end of each trading day all transactions must be settled, or offsetting contracts executed.

A commodities trader, much like a stockbroker, buys a seat on a trading exchange. The principal ones, all subject to regulation by the federal Commodity Futures Trading Commission, are the Chicago Board of Trade (corn, oats, soybeans, wheat, gold, and silver); the Chicago Mercantile Exchange (cattle, hogs, pork bellies, broilers [chickens], and lumber); the New York Commodity Exchange (gold, silver, and copper); the New York Mercantile Exchange (platinum, palladium, crude oil, heating oil, gasoline, propane, and natural gas); the New York Coffee, Sugar, and Cocoa Exchange; the Kansas City Board of Trade (wheat and sorghum [cereal or sugar grasses]); the Minneapolis Grain Exchange (wheat); the Winnipeg Commodity Exchange (wheat, canola oil, barley, and flaxseed); the MidAmerica Commodity Exchange (cattle, hogs, corn, soybeans, wheat, and silver); the Chicago Rice and Cotton Exchange; and the New York Cotton Exchange.

Each contract involves a specific quantity of the commodity. For example, some of the grain contracts are for 5,000 bushels, others for 40,000 pounds. Precious-metal contracts are measured in 50, 100, 1,000, or 5,000 troy ounces. Crude oil contracts are for 1,000 barrels, refined gasoline for 42,000 gallons. All other commodities have their own benchmark weights or quantities for each contract.

The contracts have an expiration date set by the ex-

Q My investment manager and account representative have recommended that I allow them to exercise options to improve my
portfolio. While I have confidence in them, I know nothing about
puts and calls. This portfolio represents an important portion of my
retirement fund. Should I accept their advice?

A Put-and-call trading is a very technical investment technique
that is supposedly a guarantee against excessive losses. Many
mutual funds use this strategy, but I don't see them leading the
pack—except, possibly, in the highest-management-fee category.
There is a saying that if you don't understand, don't invest. I agree.
Will you still have confidence in these advisers if the necessary extra
trading commissions and volatile markets reduce your retirement nest
egg? Whenever big gains are to be made, there is also the possibility
of big losses.

Q Are investments in gold stocks, gold mining, gold bullion,
and/or gold mutual funds sound investments?

A Only the fearful or the hoarder buys gold bullion. It pays no
dividend, has to be safely stored at a cost, and incurs endless
commissions. If you want to invest in precious metals, stick to mutual
funds or individual mining stocks. Either will be less expensively
managed, and the stocks will reflect current bullion prices, may pay
dividends, and may have the potential for capital gains.

changes, some every month and others at the end of multiple
months. Both hedgers and speculators trade on margin or,
more simply, put up a fraction, varying from 5 to 10 percent
of the face value of the contract. It is only on settlement date
that any profit or loss is realized and any exchange of cash and
commodity occurs. The end user of the commodity will actually be buying in the cash market, but in this side market the

hedger is protecting him- or herself against price volatility, and the speculator is gambling on realizing a profit by selling the contract at a higher price before the expiration date.

In more recent years the Chicago Mercantile Exchange's International Monetary Market and the New York Cotton Exchange's Financial Instrument Exchange created similar financial futures contracts for trading in foreign currencies. These hedges were particularly important for U.S. companies juggling exchange rates to bring home profits earned overseas or other opportunities for investment speculators.

The success of such earlier futures trading led to the introduction of a wide variety of other derivative securities, of which common-stock options are the most popular for professional and institutional investors.

The Chicago Board of Trade was again the leader in registering and trading stock options, beginning in 1977. The regional exchanges, particularly the AMEX, the Philadelphia, and the Pacific stock exchanges, saw this as an opportunity to increase their trading volumes and by 1980 had listed about 300 common-stock options, mostly those trading on the New York Stock Exchange. These listings fall under the regulatory jurisdiction of the Securities and Exchange Commission.

Each option contract represents one hundred shares of the underlying common stock or a bundling of common stocks such as the S&P 500 Index. An option has two components, a *put* and a *call*. A put is the right to sell the underlying stock, presumably owned or controlled by the trader, at a certain price until a certain expiration date. A call is the right to buy the underlying stock at a certain price until the expiration date of the contract. If the underlying stock is trading near or at expiration time for less than the *option exercise price*, a call holder naturally will not bother exercising the right to buy, and the contract will expire worthless. The call buyer will lose his or her investment, and the put trader will pocket the profit. These contracts trade continuously, with the traders and the investors realizing fractional profits or losses with daily price settlements handled by the Options Clearing Corp.

The availability of common-stock option futures has led to what is called *program trading*. In these transactions, an institutional investor will sell all (or a set portion) of the common stocks in his or her portfolio and simultaneously buy futures contracts in the same stocks. Or if the portfolio includes proportionately the same number of shares included in the S&P 500 Stock Index, an institutional investor may swap from common-stock holdings to the same investment in an S&P futures contract. This results in very quick and volatile changes in the day's market trend, usually in the last hour of trading.

Some days, by the same single trading order, the institutional investor may switch multimillion-dollar portfolios from the futures contract back to purchase of the actual common stocks. Occasionally the stock options, the index options, and the futures contracts all expire on the same day, often on a Friday. This results in what is called the *triple witching hour*, when there is unusually high volume and rapid changes in the market prices of the common stocks.

Some contracts involve what are called *naked* options, simply meaning that the traders neither own nor control the underlying stocks, and if their trading-price guess is wrong, they must buy the stock on its regular trading exchange at a loss and deliver to the winning option buyer. This is one expensive trap that many investors fall into when they give their broker discretionary authority to trade their account at will. The broker may hope he can make a killing, or at least keep your investment portfolio intact, but too often he loses, and the only gain is his own commissions.

Another risky—or profitable—investment tactic is what is called *short-selling*. The short-seller borrows stock through her broker, sells those shares at the day's trading price, and then waits to see when she can buy the stocks back at a lower price and return the borrowed shares to the broker. This could occur the next day, week, month, or whenever. In the meantime the registered owner gets any dividends declared and continues to vote any proxy statements. If you have the stocks in your portfolio held in street name with a broker, it is not unlikely that those shares are periodically loaned to short-sellers for a fee paid to the broker. This, of course, also involves a risk to the brokerage house. If the shares trade at a higher price than they did when they were loaned to the short-seller, both she and the broker must buy back the shares at a higher price. Often, though, the trading price of the stock does fall, and the short-seller buys replacement shares and profits from the price difference.

Once a month *The Wall Street Journal* publishes three lists on alternate days of those common stocks listed on the NYSE, AMEX, and NASDAQ-NMS for which there are 10,000 or more shares held in *short interest*. This shows the total number of borrowed shares outstanding compared with the previous month. A higher *open interest* presumably indicates that more investors think the stock price is going down further or, obversely, how many more shares will have to be bought if the stock price starts to go up.

Limited partnerships (LPs) and real estate investment trusts (REITs) are other familiar investments to be avoided by the novice. These issues were designed purely to help individuals evade tax liabilities. The issuing general partners switch corporate assets (such as commercial real estate or oil and gas holdings) to a separate entity (the partnership) and annually transfer any profits and all deductible costs of doing business to the limited partners, the investors who bought the original partnership shares. The general partners hold about 10 or 15 percent of the original issue and pay no federal taxes, but collect a healthy annual management fee and are accountable to no other shareholder. Stockbrokers and financial planners energetically sold these high-commission issues in the late 1970s and early 1980s, particularly to older investors who had little understanding of the corporate structure but were lured by the chance for tax credits and a supposedly big payoff five to ten years down the road.

When Congress revoked the tax credits in 1984, many LP investors awoke to the reality of collapsed real estate and energy markets and discovered there was no way to sell their shares nor anyone able to quote a going price, except those very few brokerage houses that had agreed in advance to try and match a seller and a buyer. Even then an investor lost a substantial amount of the initial investment. The only exceptions to this short-lived racket were and are those few LPs and REITs listed and actively trading on a stock exchange. The per-share prices are quoted daily, and an investor can find a market maker to bail out anytime, albeit often at a loss. Millions of dollars invested in LPs and REITs have been lost forever, and only the well-paid general partners and eager salesmen benefited.

So-called penny stocks are one more popular investment a novice should avoid. Most are undisguised scams with the underwriter brokers being the only market makers—and too often stock-price riggers. This is not to suggest that an infinitesimal number don't eventually gain in value and status.

But remember back a few years, when it was considered that uranium, needed for nuclear bombs and the still-to-come rash of nuclear power plants, was in short supply. Scores of penny stocks for western mining companies were issued through underwriters trading on smaller stock exchanges in Colorado, Nevada, and Utah. Most now are defunct, and gullible public investors have lost vast sums.

Similarly, every section of the country has its quota of penny-stock brokers promoting stock in companies that disappear very quickly. It is easy to buy a few thousand shares at these prices but very difficult to find a buyer should you want to sell. So any inclination to invest this way should be considered as a crapshoot—sometimes you win, but more often the house broker is the only winner.

20

Be Your Own Expert

I f you have read this far you surely know investing is not child's play, but I hope it has been sufficiently demystified that you will feel confident to try managing your own savings. Even the experts can't do any better all the time. In fact, an abbreviated review of the 1991 stock market ups and downs pinpoints divergent expert opinions.

The year started with the Dow Jones Industrial Average (DJIA) at 2633.66. By year end the figure was 3168.83, for a gain of 535.17 points, or 20 percent. None of the market experts quoted in the daily financial press had dreamed there would be such a runup. New highs of the popular DJIA were registered in February, March, April, June, August, and October. The year's final leap came in December, when the Federal Reserve Bank dropped its *discount rate* (what it charges for loans to member banks) by a full 1 percent to 3.5 percent, or half the rate charged twelve months previous.

Each time the DJIA set new lows in February, March, April, May, June, August, October, November, and early December, the market experts were quoted as alternately blaming low corporate earnings reports, the latest government job and production statistics, the failure of the Federal Reserve to cut interest rates, etc., etc.

The very morning (Friday, December 20) that the Federal Reserve ordered its full 1 percent interest rate cut, *The Wall Street Journal*'s stock market summary (written the previous night) noted: "Analysts said investors have about given up hope that the Federal Reserve will cut short-term interest rates before Christmas."

The next day's follow-up story, reporting a market response of a 20.12 point increase in the DJIA, also included pro and con quotations from nationally known financial market experts. One said: "My best guess is that after the one-day flash, you go back to reality, and reality has not changed all that much. We have a sluggish economy and a rather high valuation on stocks." Another said: "The doctor (the Fed) keeps putting penicillin into the patient, but the patient's not responding." In the meantime the Dow Jones index continued to climb, registering a 254.47 point gain through year end and was still climbing through the first week of the New Year.

Not even the most optimistic market analysts expect stock market prices to increase uninterrupted, but one of the industry's canny forecasters said that weekend that she expected "we can go up 20 percent (to a DJIA of about 3500) from here over the next twelve months."

The only reason to recount these different views is to show that even those who direct multibillion-dollar portfolios can be just as wrong as any investor. I recall a group interview years ago with Walter Wriston, then chairman of Citicorp, the nation's largest commericial bank. He was asked for his reaction to the latest forecast by economist Henry Kaufman, the then-preeminent analyst of interest-rate trends for Salomon Brothers. The banker smiled and replied, "Henry is right half the time and sometimes wrong the other half; but anyone who bats .500 can play on my team!" That's a philosophical attitude worth remembering—your guess can sometimes be as valid as those of recognized experts. My classic example of contrary stock story quotes is this: "The market didn't go up, so it went down," said one brokerage executive when asked to comment on that day's dull action. Translated, what he really was saying is that neither news nor professional investors spurred higher prices, so the lemmings started selling. A novice investor should ignore the daily ups and downs of the market.

Earlier I recommended *One Up on Wall Street* by Peter Lynch as a handy all-around instructive book for novice investors. His chapter on *Designing a Portfolio*, is especially informative for those tempted to follow current investing fads. He doesn't think much of trying to time the market by switching from stocks to cash and vice versa. He writes: "My idea is to stay in the market forever, and to rotate stocks depending on the fundamental situations. I think if you decide that a certain amount you've invested in the stock market always will be invested in the stock market, you'll save yourself a lot of mistimed moves and general agony. If a stalwart [stock] has gone up 40 percent—which is all I expected to get out of it—and nothing wonderful has happened with the company to make me think there are pleasant surprises ahead, I sell the stock and replace it with another stalwart.... As long as the original story (your reason for buying) continues to make sense, or gets better, you'll be amazed at the results in several years."

Of course, Lynch's guidelines to successful investing are of more use to a portfolio manager than a novice investor. His search for the "fundamental story" of a stock was greatly enhanced by his ability to command the limitless talent of Fidelity's research staff and his freedom to get personal access to corporate managers at distant headquarters. If you or I wanted to ask a busy corporate CEO tough questions about the company's health and stock prospects, we wouldn't even get an appointment, let alone any useful information. But who could ignore the manager of a multibillion-dollar stock portfolio?

Nevertheless, *One Up on Wall Street* is chock-full of entertaining, interesting, and helpful information presented in language comprehensible to the novice investor. The following tips are particularly useful:
- the key numbers to look for in a company's annual report
- understanding a company's debt-to-equity ratio and isolating its cash-flow figures
- interpreting the price/earnings ratio numbers
- a five-point checklist for selecting stocks
- the ideal portfolio size—three to ten stocks
- when to sell different categories of stock

Here's my own short list of cardinal investing rules:
- decide and stick to your own risk tolerance.
- always have a percentage of investable funds in common stocks to keep pace with inflation.
- buy stocks of high-quality companies.
- ignore daily price changes; invest for the long term.
- consider any speculative buys as crapshoot money.
- fully fund any available tax-deferred retirement accounts.
- consider time spent learning about investments as profitable fun.

Appendix A

Federal Reserve Banks handling purchase and redemption of U.S. Treasury securities. (In most cases the second telephone listing is for an informational recording only.)

Federal Reserve Bank of Atlanta, P.O. Box 1731, Atlanta, GA 30303; (404-521-8653 or 404-521-8657).

Federal Reserve Bank of Baltimore, P.O. Box 1378, Baltimore, MD 21201; (301-576-3553 or 301-576-3500).

Federal Reserve Bank of Birmingham, P.O. Box C10447, Birmingham, AL 35283; (205-252-3141, Ext. 215 or 264).

Federal Reserve Bank of Boston, P.O. Box 2076, Boston, MA 02106; (617-973-3810 or 617-973-3805).

Federal Reserve Bank of Buffalo, P.O. Box 961, Buffalo, NY 14240; (716-849-5030 or 716-849-5158).

Federal Reserve Bank of Charlotte, P.O. Box 30248, Charlotte, NC 28230; (704-336-7267 or 704-336-7276).

Federal Reserve Bank of Chicago, P.O. Box 834, Chicago, IL 60690; (312-322-5369 or 312-786-1110).

Federal Reserve Bank of Cincinnati, P.O. Box 999, Cincinnati, OH 45201; (513-721-4787, Ext. 333).

Federal Reserve Bank of Cleveland, P.O. Box 6387, Cleveland, OH 44101; (216-579-2490).

Federal Reserve Bank of Dallas, Securities Dept., Station K, Dallas, TX 75222; (214-651-6362 or 214-651-6177).

Federal Reserve Bank of Denver, P.O. Box 5228, Terminal Annex, Denver, CO 80217; (303-572-2477 or 303-572-2475).

Federal Reserve Bank of Detroit, P.O. Box 1059, Detroit, MI 48231; (313-964-6157 or 6158 or 313-963-0080).

Federal Reserve Bank of El Paso, P.O. Box 100, El Paso, TX 79999; (214-651-6362 or 214-651-6177).

Federal Reserve Bank of Houston, P.O. Box 2578, Houston, TX 77252; (713-659-4433 or 713-652-1688).

Federal Reserve Bank of Jacksonville, P.O. Box 2499, Jacksonville, FL 32231; (904-632-1179).

Federal Reserve Bank of Kansas City, Securities Dept., P.O. Box 440, Kansas City, MO 64198; (816-881-2783 or 2409 or 816-881-2767).

Federal Reserve Bank of Little Rock, P.O. Box 1261, Little Rock, AR 72203; (501-372-5451, Ext. 288).

Federal Reserve Bank of Los Angeles, P.O. Box 2077, Terminal Annex, Los Angeles, CA 90051; (213-624-7398 or 213-688-0068).

Federal Reserve Bank of Louisville, P.O. Box 32710, Louisville, KY 40232; (502-568-9236 or 9231).

Federal Reserve Bank of Memphis, P.O. Box 407, Memphis, TN 38101; (901-523-7171, Ext. 225 or 641).

Federal Reserve Bank of Miami, P.O. Box 520847, Miami, FL 33152; (305-591-2065).

Federal Reserve Bank of Minneapolis, 250 Marquette Avenue, Minneapolis, MN 55480; (612-340-2075).

Federal Reserve Bank of Nashville, 301 Eighth Avenue North, Nashville, TN 37203; (615-259-4006, Ext. 261).

Federal Reserve Bank of New Orleans, P.O. Box 61630, New Orleans, LA 70161; (504-586-1505, Ext. 293).

Federal Reserve Bank of New York, Federal Reserve Post Office Station, New York, NY 10045; (212-720-6619 or 212-720-7773).

Federal Reserve Bank of Oklahoma City, P.O. Box 25129, Oklahoma City, OK 73125; (405-270-8652).

Federal Reserve Bank of Omaha, 2201 Farnam Street, Omaha, NE 68102; (402-221-5633).

Federal Reserve Bank of Philadelphia, P.O. Box 66, Philadelphia, PA 19105; (215-574-6675).

Federal Reserve Bank of Pittsburgh, P.O. Box 867, Pittsburgh, PA 15230-0867; (412-261-7863 or 412-261-7988).

Federal Reserve Bank of Portland, P.O. Box 3436, Portland, OR 97208; (503-221-5932 or 503-221-5921).

Federal Reserve Bank of Richmond, P.O. Box 27622, Richmond, VA 23261-7622; (804-697-8372 or 804-697-8355).

Federal Reserve Bank of Salt Lake City, P.O. Box 30780, Salt Lake City, UT 84130; (801-322-7944 or 801-322-7911).

Federal Reserve Bank of San Antonio, P.O. Box 1471, San Antonio, TX 78295; (512-224-2141, Ext. 303 or 311).

Federal Reserve Bank of San Francisco, P.O. Box 7702, San Francisco, CA 94120; (415-974-2330 or 415-882-9798).

Federal Reserve Bank of Seattle, P.O. Box 3567, Seattle, WA 98124; (206-442-1652 or 206-442-1650).

Federal Reserve Bank of St. Louis, P.O. Box 442, St. Louis, MO 63166; (314-444-8506 or 314-444-8602).

Source: *Buying Treasury Securities at Federal Reserve Banks* by James T. Tucker, published by the Federal Reserve Bank of Richmond.

Appendix B

The Major United States
and Canadian Stock Markets

AMEX—American Stock Exchange, 86 Trinity Place, New
York, NY 10006 (212-306-1406).

NASDAQ/NMS—National Association of Securities Dealers
Automated Quotations, National Market System, 1735 K
Street NW, Washington, D.C. 20006 (202-728-8000).

NYSE—New York Stock Exchange, 11 Wall Street, New
York, NY 10005 (212-656-3000).

The Regional Exchanges

Boston Stock Exchange, One Boston Place, Boston, MA
02108 (617-723-9500).

Cincinnati Stock Exchange, 49 East Fourth Street, Cincinnati, OH 45202 (513-621-1410).

Midwest Stock Exchange, 440 South LaSalle Street, Chicago, IL 60605 (312-663-2279).

Pacific Stock Exchange, 301 Pine Street, San Francisco, CA 94104 (415-393-4000); and the second trading floor, 233 South Beaudry, Los Angeles, CA 90012 (213-977-4500).

Philadelphia Stock Exchange, 1900 Market Street, Philadelphia, PA 19103 (215-496-5214).

Canadian Exchanges

Alberta Stock Exchange, 300 Fifth Avenue S.W., Calgary, Alberta, T2P 3C4 (403-262-7791).

Montreal Stock Exchange, Stock Exchange Tower, 800 Victoria Square, Montreal, Quebec H4Z 1A9 (514-871-2424).

Toronto Stock Exchange, 2 First Canadian Place, Toronto, Ontario, M5X 1J2 (416-947-4514).

Vancouver Stock Exchange, 609 Granville Street, P.O. Box 10333, Vancouver, B.C. V7Y 1H1 (604-689-3334).

Winnipeg Stock Exchange, 2901 One Lombard Place, Winnipeg, Manitoba R3B 0Y2 (204-942-8431).

Source: Standard & Poor's *Securities Dealers of North America*.

Appendix C

State Securities Administrators

These officials, variously named administrators, commissioners, or directors, supervise the incoporation of stock-issuing companies and regulate the sale of any stocks, bonds, and mutual funds within their states and provinces.

Alabama—Securities Commission, 770 Washington Avenue, Montgomery, AL 36130 (205-242-2984).

Alaska—Division of Banking Securities & Corporations, Department of Commerce & Economic Development, P.O. Box D, State Office Building, Juneau, AK 99811 (907-465-2521).

Arizona—Securities Division, Arizona Corporation Commission, 1200 West Washington, Phoenix, AZ 85007 (602-542-0644).

Arkansas—Securities Commission, Heritage West Building, 201 East Markham, Little Rock, AR 72201 (501-324-9260).

California—Corporations Commission, 3700 Wilshire Boulevard, Los Angeles, CA 90010 (213-736-2741).

Colorado—Division of Securities, 1580 Lincoln Street, Denver, CO 80203 (303-894-2320).

Connecticut—Securities & Business Investment Division, Department of Banking, 44 Capitol Avenue, Hartford, CT 06106 (203-566-4560).

Delaware—Division of Securities, Deptartment of Justice, Carvel Office Building, 820 North French Street, Wilmington, DE 19801 (302-577-2515).

District of Columbia—Office of Securities, Public Service Commission, 450 5th Street NW, Washington, D.C. 20001 (202-626-5105).

Florida—Division of Securities & Investor Protection, The Capitol, Tallahassee, FL 32399 (904-488-9805).

Georgia—Secretary of State, Business Service & Regulation, 2 Martin Luther King Jr. Drive, Atlanta, GA (404-656-2895).

Hawaii—Commissioner of Securities, 1010 Richards Street, P.O. Box 40, Honolulu, HI 96810 (808-548-2744).

Idaho—Department of Finance, 700 West State Street, Boise, ID 83720 (208-334-3313).

Illinois—Director of Securities, 900 South Spring Street, Springfield, IL 62704 (217-782-2256); or 188 West Randolph, Chicago, IL 60601 (312-793-3384).

Indiana—Securities Commission, 302 West Washington, Indianapolis, IN 46204 (317-232-6681).

Iowa—Securities Bureau, Lucas State Office Building, Des Moines, IA 50319 (515-281-4441).

Kansas—Securities Commission, 618 South Kansas Avenue, Topeka, KS 66603 (913-296-3307).

Kentucky—Division of Securities, 911 Leawood Drive, Frankfort, KY 40601 (502-564-3390).

Louisiana—Securities Commission, Louisiana State Office Building, 325 Loyola Avenue, New Orleans, LA 70112 (504-568-5515).

Maine—Securities Division, State House Station 121, Augusta, ME 04333 (207-582-8760).

Maryland—Division of Securities, 200 St. Paul Place, Baltimore, MD 21202 (301-576-6360).

Massachusetts—Secretary of the Commonwealth, Securities Division, One Ashburton Place, Boston, MA 02108 (617-727-3548).

Michigan—Department of Commerce, Corporation & Securities Bureau, P.O. Box 30222, Lansing, MI 48909 (517-334-6206).

Minnesota—Commerce Commission, 133 East 7th Street, St. Paul, MN 55101 (612-296-6325).

Mississippi—Secretary of State, Securities Division, 401 Mississippi Street, P.O. Box 136, Jackson, MS 39205 (601-359-6371).

Missouri—Secretary of State, Securities Division, 301 West High Street, Truman State Office Building, Jefferson City, MO 65101 (314-751-4136).

Montana—Securities Commission, P.O. Box 4009, Helena, MT 59604 (406-444-2040).

Nebraska—Department of Banking & Finance, Bureau of Securities, 301 Centennial Mall South, P.O. Box 95006, Lincoln, NE 68509 (402-471-3445).

Nevada—Secretary of State, Securities Division, 2501 East Sahara Avenue, Las Vegas, NV 89158 (702-486-4400).

New Hampshire—Office of Securities Regulation, 157 Manchester Street, Concord, NH 03301 (603-271-1463).

New Jersey—Bureau of Securities, Two Gateway Center, Newark, NJ 07102 (201-648-2040).

New Mexico—Securities Division, 725 St. Michaels Drive, Santa Fe, NM 87501 (505-827-7140).

New York—Investor Protection & Securities Bureau, 120 Broadway, New York, NY 10271 (212-341-2200).

North Carolina—Securities Division, 300 North Salisbury Street, Raleigh, NC 27611 (919-733-3924).

North Dakota—Securities Commission, 600 East Boulevard, State Capitol, Bismarck, ND 58505 (701-224-2910).

Ohio—Division of Securities, 77 South High Street, Columbus, OH 43266 (614-644-7381).

Oklahoma—Department of Securities, Will Rogers Memorial Office Building, P.O. Box 53595, Oklahoma City, OK 73152 (405-521-2451).

Oregon—Division of Finance & Securities, 21 Labor & Industries Building, Salem, OR 97310 (503-378-4387).

Pennsylvania—Securities Commission, Eastgate Office Building, 1010 North 7th Street, Harrisburg, PA 17102 (717-787-8061).

Rhode Island—Superintendent of Securities, 233 Richmond Street, Providence, RI 02903 (401-277-3048).

South Carolina—Securities Commission, Edgar Brown Building, 1205 Pendleton Street, Columbia, SC 29201 (803-734-1087).

South Dakota—Division of Securities, 910 East Sioux Avenue, Pierre, SD 57501 (605-773-4823).

Tennessee—Securities Commission, Department of Commerce & Insurance, 500 James Robertson Parkway, Nashville, TN 37243 (615-741-5911).

Texas—Securities Commission, 1800 San Jacinto, P.O. Box 13167, Capitol Station, Austin, TX 78711 (512-474-2233).

Utah—Securities Division, Heber M. Wells Building, 160 East 300 South, P.O. Box 45808, Salt Lake City, UT 84145 (801-530-6600).

Vermont—Department of Banking, Insurance & Securities, Montpelier, VT 06520 (802-828-3420).

Virginia—Division of Securities, 1220 Bank Street, P.O. Box 1197, Richmond, VA 23209 (804-786-7751).

Washington—Securities Division, P.O. Box 9033, Olympia, WA 98507 (206-753-6928).

West Virginia—Securities Commission, State Capitol Building, Charleston, WV 25305 (304-348-2257).

Wisconsin—Securities Commission, 111 West Wilson Street, P.O. Box 1768, Madison, WI 53701 (608-266-3431).

Wyoming—Secretary of State, Securities Administration, Capitol Building, Cheyenne, WY 82002 (307-777-7370).

Canadian Administrators

Alberta—Securities Commission, 10025 Jasper Avenue, Edmonton, Alberta T5J 3Z5 (403-422-1083) or 410-300-5th Avenue S.W., Calgary, Alberta T2P 3C4 (403-297-4277).

British Columbia—Securities Commission, 1100-865 Hornby Street, Vancouver, B.C. V6Z 2H4 (604-660-4800).

Manitoba—Securities Commission, 1128-405 Broadway Avenue, Winnipeg, Manitoba R3C 3L6 (204-945-2550).

Ontario—Securities Commission, 20 Queen Street W., P.O. Box 55, Toronto, Ontario M5H 3S8 (416-593-8156).

Quebec—Securities Commission, C.P. 246, Tour de la Bourse, Montreal, Quebec H4Z I3G (514-873-5326).

Saskatchewan—Securities Commission, 850-1914 Hamilton Street, Regina, Saskatchewan S4P 3V7 (306-787-5645).

Source: Standard & Poor's *Securities Dealers of North America.*

Appendix D

National Association of Securities Dealers

Headquarters—1735 K Street NW, Washington, D.C. 20006-1506 (202-728-8000 or 301-590-6500).

District One with jurisdiction over northern California, northern Nevada, and Hawaii—425 California Street, San Francisco, CA 94104 (415-781-3434).

District Two for southern California and southern Nevada—300 South Grand Avenue, Los Angeles, CA 90071 (213-627-2122).

District Three for Arizona, Colorado, New Mexico, Utah, and Wyoming—1401 17th Street, Denver, CO 80202 (303-298-7234).

District Three for Alaska, Idaho, Montana, Oregon, and Washington—One Union Square, 600 University, Seattle, WA 98101-3132 (206-624-0790).

District Four for Iowa, Kansas, Minnesota, Missouri, Nebraska, North Dakota, and South Dakota—12 Wyandotte Plaza, 120 West 12th Street, Kansas City, MO 64105 (816-421-5700).

District Five for Alabama, Arkansas, Kentucky, Louisiana, Mississippi, Oklahoma, and Tennessee—1100 Poydras Street, Suite 850 Energy Centre, New Orleans, LA 70163 (504-522-6527).

District Six for Texas—1999 Bryan Street, Suite 1450, Olympia & York Tower, Dallas, TX 75201 (214-969-7050).

District Seven for Florida, Georgia, North Carolina, South Carolina, Puerto Rico and Canal Zone, and the Virgin Islands—One Securities Centre, Suite 500, 3490 Piedmont Road N.E., Atlanta, GA 30305 (404-239-6100).

District Eight for Illinois, Indiana, Michigan, and Wisconsin—10 South LaSalle Street, Chicago, IL 60603-1002 (312-899-4400).

District Eight for Ohio and part of upstate New York—Renaissance on Playhouse Square, 1350 Euclid Avenue, Cleveland, OH 44115 (216-694-4545).

District Nine for Delaware, Pennsylvania, West Virgina, and southern New Jersey—1818 Market Street, Philadelphia, PA 19103 (215-665-1180).

District Nine for District of Columbia, Maryland, and Virginia—1735 K Street NW, Washington, D.C. 20006-1506 (202-728-8400).

District Ten for the five boroughs of New York City and adjacent counties and northern New Jersey—33 Whitehall Street, New York, NY 10004 (212-858-4000).

District Eleven for Connecticut, Maine, Massachusetts, New Hampshire, Rhode Island, Vermont, and New York (except those areas under jurisdiction of District Ten)—260 Franklin Street, Boston, MA 02110 (617-261-0800).

Regional Arbitration Offices

New York—NASD Financial Center, 33 Whitehall Street, New York, NY 10004 (212-480-4881).

California—425 California Street, Room 1400, San Francisco, CA 94104 (415-781-3343).

Florida—One East Broward Boulevard, Suite 1000, Fort Lauderdale, FL 33301 (305-522-7391).

Illinois—10 South LaSalle Street, 20th Floor, Chicago, IL 60603-1002 (312-899-4440).

Source: Standard & Poor's *Securities Dealers of North America.*

INDEX

A

AAII Journal, 111
Age, and choice of investments, 58, 67–68, 117–18, 133–34
Aggressive Growth mutual fund, 58
AMBAC Indemnity Corporation, 78
American Association of Individual Investors, 111
American Depositary Receipts (ADRs)
  dividend payments, 47
  nature of, 46–47, 48
  tax aspects, 47
American Stock Exchange (AMEX)
  Emerging Company Marketplace, 54
  listing requirements, 28–29
  Market Value Index, 99
Ask price
  mutual funds, 63
  over-the-counter market, 51, 52

B

Balanced mutual fund, 58, 133–34
Banker's acceptances, 20

Bank failure, and certificates of deposit, 13
Bank Rate Monitor, CD information, 11, 14–15
Bank trust services, 133
Barron's, 86, 90, 93, 107, 135
  as information source, 107–8
Barron's/Lipper Index, 60, 108
Bearer bonds, 74
Better Investing, 111–12
Bid price
  mutual funds, 63
  over-the-counter market, 51, 52
Big Board, 30, 31
Bonds
  corporate bonds, 79, 82–83
  early call dates, 73–74
  government bonds, 80–81
  investment grade, 74
  municipal bonds, 76–79
  rating of, 74–76
  secondary bond investments, 79–80
  unit investment trust (UIT), 77–78
Book entry, 3
Broker
  discount broker, 70, 115–16
  disputes with brokerage, 121–22
  establishing account with, 116

full-service accounts, advantages of, 119–20
selection of, 120–21
use of, 70, 115
Broker's loan rate, 119
Bulletin Board, OTC securities, 52, 54

C

Call dates, bonds, 73–74
Cash sweep, 119
Certificates of deposit (CDs), 9–15
and bank failure, 13
Bank Rate Monitor information, 11, 14–15
guarantee regulations, 12, 13
insured CDs, 9
interest rates, 10, 12
maximum investment, 9–10, 12
tax aspects, 12
Chicago Board of Trade, 146, 148
Closed-end funds
country funds, 85–86
initial offering of, 87
mutual funds, 56
trading quotation, 88–89
Commercial paper, 21
Commodities, 145–48
futures contracts, nature of, 146–48
hedgers and speculators, 145–46
trading exchanges, 146
Common stock quotation pages, 35–42
cash dividends in dollars, 36
name of stock, 36
price/earnings ratio, 37
price ranges for trades, 38
Standard & Poor's *Stock Guide*, 35–39
symbols used, 39, 41
Wall Street Journal, 35, 39–41
yesterday's trading figures, 37–38
yield, 36–37
Common stocks, 25–33
AMEX listing requirements, 28–29
dividends, 25, 36
Dow Jones Industrial Average, 31–32
initial public offering, 26
NASDAQ listing requirements, 29–30
nature of, 25–26
NYSE listing requirements, 26–28
par value, 26
and regional stock exchanges, 30–31
split shares, 27, 39
trading information, omissions in, 31–33
Contingent deferred sales charge, 62
Convertible bonds, 79

Convertible feature, preferred stock, 44
Corporate bonds, 79
  nature of, 79
  trading quotations, 82–83
Country funds, 85
  discount trading, 86
  information sources on, 90
  nature of, 85, 86
  quotation information, 86

D

Debentures, 80
Defensive rights, 46
Directory of Companies Offering Reinvestment Plans, 71
Discount broker, 70
  selection of, 115–16
Discount rate, 10, 153
Diversification, 68
  recommendations for, 58
Dividend reinvestment plans (DRIPs)
  information sources about, 71
  nature of, 71
Dividends
  American Depositary Receipts (ADRs), 47
  common stock, 25, 36
  dividend reports, 101–2
  ex-dividend, 102–3
  preferred stock, 43, 44
  reinvestment of, 118
Donoghue Report, 19

Donoghue's Money Fund Report, 19
Donoghue's Mutual Funds Almanac, 59–60
  as information source, 109–10
Dow Jones Industrial Average, 31–32, 91–96, 153–54
  companies of, 94–95
  components of, 92
Transportation and Utilities averages, 95–96

E

Emerging Company Marketplace, AMEX, 54
Equipment leasing bonds, 79
Eurodollars, 21
Ex-dividend, 38
  and buying and selling shares, 102–3
  listing of trading ex-dividend, 103–5
meaning of, 63

F

Fannie Maes, 81
Federal Deposit Insurance Corporation (FDIC), 9, 12, 13, 24
Federal funds rate, 10, 11
Federal Reserve Banks, 2
  listing of, 157–60
Financial Guarantee Insurance Co., 79

Fitch, Duff & Phelps, 20
Floating rate notes, 21
Forbes, 60, 107
  as information source, 108–9
401(k) plans, 140
  types of, 140
403(b) plans, 140, 141
Freddie Macs, 81
Full-load funds, 62
Full-service brokerage accounts,
  advantages of, 119–20

G

Ginnie Maes, 81
Gold, 147
Government-agency bonds,
  80–81
  types of, 81
Growth and Income mutual
  fund, 58
Guaranteed investment contract, 140
Guide to Mutual Funds, 59
  as information source, 109

I

*IBC/Donoghue's Money Fund Re-
  port*, 14, 19, 20, 21
Index funds, 98
Individual Retirement Accounts
  (IRA), 137–40
  age of withdrawal, 138
  best investment vehicles for,
  138

  tax liability, 138–39
Inherited securities
  appraisal of portfolio, 130,
  132
  finding cost basis for, 124,
  131
  old securities, sources of information on, 134–36
  redirecting investments,
  132–33
  reregistration of certificates,
  129–30
Initial public offering, 26, 46
Institutional investors, 2–3,
  55–56
  types of, 56
Insurance proceeds, investment
  of, 130
International Bank Credit Anal-
  ysis, 20
Investing
  age and investment goals, 58,
  67–68
  basic guidelines for, 156
  basic issues in, 55
  brokers, 70, 115–16
  dealing with fluctuations, 70
  diversification, 58, 68
  dividend reinvestment plans
  (DRIPs), 71
  information sources for tracking markets, 107–13
  investment clubs, 71–72
  program trading, effects on
  investors, 55
  retirement accounts, 137–43

risky investments, types of, 145–52
Investment clubs, 71–72
organization for, 71, 111–12

J

Junk bonds, 80

L

Limited partnerships, 150–51
Limit order, 117
Lipper Analytical Services, mutual fund performance, 60–61
Loads, types for mutual funds, 61–62
Low-load funds, 62

M

Margin calls, 119
Market order, 117
Merrill, Lynch Inc., money-market funds, 22–24
MONEYLETTER, 110
Money market funds, 17–24
bank funds, 24
nature of, 17–19
publication on, 19–21
safety factors, 18
sweep accounts, 21, 24
taxable funds, types of holdings in, 20–21
tax aspects, 24
tax-free funds, 18, 19, 22, 24
types of, 22–23
Moneypaper, 71
Moody's Investor Services, 20
bond ratings, 74, 75
Municipal Bond Investors Assurance Corporation, 78
Municipal bonds, 76–79
nature of, 76–77
purchase of, 77
safety factor, 78–79
tax aspects, 76
Mutual funds, 55–65
Aggressive Growth/Capital Appreciation funds, 58
Balanced fund, 58
closed-end funds, 56
ex-dividend date, 102–3
Growth and Income/Equity-Income fund, 58
information sources on, 59–61
investment goals and fund selection, 58
loads, types of, 61–62
mutual fund chart, interpretation of, 62–65
open-end funds, 56
prospectus of, 56, 58
reinvestment of dividends, 118
rise of, 56
socially responsible funds, 57

N

Naked options, 149
NASDAQ
  Company Directory, 53
  Composite Index, 99–100
  Fact Book and Company Directory, 53
  listing requirements, 29–30
  over-the-counter stocks, 52–53
National Association of Investment Clubs, 71, 111–12
National Association of Securities Dealers (NASD), 26
National Credit Union Association (NCUA), 9, 13
National Stock Summary, 135
Net asset value, mutual funds, 63
New York Stock Exchange (NYSE)
  Composite Index, 98–99
  listing requirements, 26–28
No-load funds, 61, 118, 133

O

100 Highest Yield, 11
One Up on Wall Street, 112, 155–56
Only Other Investment Guide You'll Ever Need, The, 112
Open-end funds, 85
  mutual funds, 56

Open interest, 150
Over-the-counter markets, 51–54
  listing requirements, 52–54
  listings of companies, 52, 53, 54
  nature of companies on, 51, 53
  pink and yellow sheets, 52
  purchase of shares, 51–52

P

Par value, common stocks, 26
Penny stocks, 151–52
Pink sheets, over-the-counter market, 52, 53
Precious metals, 147
Preferred stock
  compared to common stock, 45
  convertible feature, 44
  dividends, 43, 44
  nature of, 43–44
Price/earnings ratio, in common stock quotation, 37
Prime rate, effect on interest rate, 11
Program trading, 55, 98
  and stock options, 149
Prospectus, of mutual fund, 56, 58
Proxy statements, 69
Put-and-call trading, 147, 148

Q

Quarterly reports, 69

R

Random Walk Down Wall Street, A, 112
Real estate investment trusts (REITs), 150–51
Record date, 102, 104
Record keeping, 123–27
  for acquisitions by tender of- fers, 127
  and dividend reinvestment plans, 125–25
  purchase statements, 124
  for retirement accounts, 124
  stock splits, 126–27
  transaction statements, 116–17
Regional stock exchanges, 30–31
Repurchase agreements, 20
Retirement accounts, 137–43
  401(k) plans, 140
  403(b) plans, 140, 141
  Individual Retirement Ac- counts, 137–40
  options for distributions, 141
  record keeping for, 124
  retirement accounts, 137–43
  United States Savings Bonds, 141–43

Rights
  defensive rights, 46
  nature of, 46
Risky investments
  commodities, 145–48
  limited partnerships, 150–51
  penny stocks, 151–52
  real estate investment trusts (REITs), 150–51
  short-selling tactic, 150
  stock options, 148–50
R.M. Smythe & Co., 136

S

Scudder-Fisher Manuals, 135
Secondary bond investments, 79–80
Secondary market, Treasury se- curities, 3, 6
Securities and Exchange Com- mission (SEC), 26
Securities Investor Protection Corporation (SIPC), 18, 78
Series EE bonds, 142
Series HH bonds, 142–43
Settlement date, 102
Short interest, 150
Short-selling, 150
Short-term corporate notes, 79
Sinking funds, 44
Small Cap listings, NASDAQ, 52, 54
Socially responsible funds, types of, 57

Split shares
  meaning of, 27, 39
  record keeping for, 126–27
Spread, over-the-counter mar-
    ket, 52
Standard & Poor's, 20
  bond ratings, 74, 75
  stock reports, 111
Standard & Poor's 500, 97–98
Standard & Poor's *Stock Guide*
  as information source, 108,
    117
  stock quotation pages, 35–39
Stock certificates, 116
Stock exchanges
  American Stock Exchange
    (AMEX), 28–29
  National Association of Secu-
    rities Dealers (NASD),
    29–30
  New York Stock Exchange
    (NYSE), 26–28
  regional, 30–31
Stock indexes
  American Stock Exchange
    Market Value Index, 99
  Dow Jones Industrial Aver-
    age, 91–96
  NASDEQ Composite Index,
    99–100
  New York Stock Exchange
    Composite Index, 98–99
  Standard & Poor's 500, 97–98
  Wilshire 5,000 Equity Index,
    100

Stock options, 148–50
  naked options, 149
  and program trading, 149
  put and call, 147, 148
Stock purchase orders, types of,
    117
Stocks. *See* Common stocks;
    Over-the-counter market;
    Preferred stock
Stop order, 117
Street-name accounts, 69, 72

T

Taxation
  American depositary receipts
    (ADRs), 47
  certificates of deposit, 12
  Individual Retirement Ac-
    counts, 138–39
  Treasury securities, 8
Tax-free funds
  money market funds, 18, 19,
    22, 24
  municipal bonds, 76
  unit investment trust (UIT),
    77–78
Tender offers in takeover,
    record keeping for, 127
Transaction statements, safe-
    keeping of, 116–17
Treasury securities, 1–8
  auction times, 1, 2
  book entry recording, 3

information source about, 8
interest rates, 2–3
newspaper information about,
    3, 6–7
purchase by institutional in-
    vestors, 2–3
purchasing of, 2
safety factor, 76, 80
secondary market, 3, 6
tax aspects, 8
T-Bills, 1, 4–5
T-Bonds, 1–2
T-Notes, 1
Treasury direct system, 3–5, 8
zero-coupon bonds, 5
Triple witching hour, 149

U

Uniform Gift to Minors Act,
    131
*United & Babson Investment Re-
    port*, 68, 110, 117
United Mutual Fund Selector, 110
United States Savings Bonds,
    141–43
purchase limit, 143
Series EE bonds, 142
Series HH bonds, 142–43
setting interest rates, 142
Unit investment trust (UIT),
    nature of, 77–78
Utilities, benefits of, 68, 133–34

V

Value Line Investment Survey, 68,
    107
as information source, 110–11

W

Wall Street Journal, 3, 86, 90,
    93, 107
as information source, 107,
    124
listing of trading ex-dividend,
    103–5
mutual fund performance, 61
short interest stock listing,
    150
stock quotation pages, 35,
    39–41
Warrants, nature of, 44, 46
Widows/widowers. *See* Inher-
    ited securities
Wilshire 5,000 Equity Index,
    100

Y

Yankeedollars, 21
Yellow sheets, over-the-counter
    market, 52

Z

Zero-coupon bonds, 5, 80

About the Author

Beatson Wallace received his B.A. degree from Harvard College, class of 1949, and did graduate studies as a Ford Foundation Traveling Fellow at the American University in Cairo, Egypt. Both during his college years and subsequently, he worked on innumerable reporting and editorial assignments at different newspapers. In December 1990 he completed thirty-nine years as a staff member of the *Boston Globe*, including ten years as business editor and ten years as a financial columnist. He is now retired and lives amid the mountains of New Hampshire.